Blue Ocean Advisor

Blue Ocean Advisor

A Step-by-Step Guide to Growing a Massive Book of Business

Chad Jenkins, Jeff Jenkins & Brian Jenkins

Copyright 2023. All Rights Reserved. No portion of this book may be reproduced, stored in a retrieval system, or transmitted in any form or by any means-electronic, mechanical, photocopy, recording, scanning, or other-except for brief quotations in critical reviews or articles without the prior permission of the author.

Published by Game Changer Publishing

Paperback ISBN: 978-1-961189-00-3
Hardcover ISBN: 978-1-961189-01-0
Digital ISBN: 978-1-961189-02-7

www.GameChangerPublishing.com

ACKNOWLEDGMENTS

We are thankful to our families for the sacrifices they had to make as we were away from home with our amazing clients while growing Blueprint into a successful business.

We are thankful to our amazing clients who have been with us for many years and helped us build out this playbook to build a massive book of business. This almost 20-year-long collaboration has been amazing, and it makes us feel very lucky to have gotten to work with all of you.

We are thankful to Cris Cawley and her team, at Game Changer Publishing, for all of her wisdom and patience as we have written this book and also for encouraging us to do so in our own voices instead of hiring a professional writer.

Last but not least, we are thankful for a loving God that would send His son to live among us and teach us that we can all flourish by simply putting others first.

A SPECIAL THANK YOU

We give a special thanks to Curtis Verstraete of OnPurpose IP, who we affectionately refer to as The Godfather. Thank you for helping us make our big ideas come to life and for coming alongside us on this journey many years ago. Your wisdom, friendship, and guidance have been invaluable.

DOWNLOAD YOUR FREE GIFTS

Read This First

Just to say thanks for buying and reading our book, we would like to give you a few free bonus gifts, no strings attached!

To Download Now, Visit:
www.BlueOceanAdvisorBook.com/Blueprintgifts

Blue Ocean Advisor

*A Step-by-Step Guide to Growing
a Massive Book of Business*

Chad Jenkins, Jeff Jenkins & Brian Jenkins

www.GameChangerPublishing.com

Preface

We wrote this book for two main reasons. The first is to help producers, new or seasoned, get in front of a lot more opportunities with their ideal clients and with a lot less effort. The second is to introduce producers to a process that helps them weed out buyers with bad intentions, stand out from their competitors, and grow a massive book of business by simply focusing on clients' goals instead of themselves. In other words, by simply helping people.

One of the biggest challenges that sales professionals face is finding the right opportunities. This can be a time-consuming and frustrating process, especially if you don't have a clear strategy for identifying and targeting your ideal clients. But with the insights and strategies outlined in this book, you can streamline your prospecting process and get in front of the right people with less effort and positioned to be different right out of the gate.

Another challenge that sales professionals face is differentiating themselves from their competitors. In a crowded marketplace, it can be difficult to stand out and demonstrate the unique value that you bring to the table. But by following the process outlined in this book, you can create a clear and compelling contrast between yourself and your competitors, making it easier for your ideal clients to choose you.

Ultimately, our goal is to help sales professionals grow a massive book of business by simply helping people. By focusing on building relationships, delivering value, and helping your clients achieve their goals, you can achieve greater success and fulfillment in your career while also positively impacting the lives of those you serve.

So if you're a sales professional looking to take your game to the next level, or if you're just starting out and want to set yourself up for success, this book is for you. We hope that the insights and strategies outlined in these pages will help you get in front of more opportunities, weed out the bad buyers, stand out from your competitors, and grow a massive book of business by simply helping people.

Table of Contents

Introduction		1
Chapter One	Why Doesn't Every Producer Have A Million-Dollar Book Of Business?	3
Chapter Two	The Foundation And Fundamentals Of Becoming A Trusted, Successful Advisor	15
Chapter Three	The Initial Meeting: What Happens When We First Meet With A Prospect?	33
Chapter Four	The Holy Grail In Sales (Discovery)	61
Chapter Five	Building A Proposal That Creates Value— The Blueprint	91
Chapter Six	The Prospecting Effectiveness Formula	101
Chapter Seven	Hidden In Plain Sight	113
Chapter Eight	Cold Calling Using A Creative Drop And How To Create A Referral Out Of Thin Air	121
Chapter Nine	Pattern Interrupt & The Three Asks	139

Introduction

There are two types of salespeople: the transactional salesperson and the trusted advisor. While both aim to close deals and generate revenue, the approach and mindset of each is vastly different. A transactional salesperson is focused on making a sale at any cost, often resorting to high-pressure tactics to push products or services onto customers. In contrast, a trusted advisor prioritizes building relationships, understanding customer needs, and providing solutions that are tailored to their unique requirements.

As the sales landscape becomes increasingly more competitive, it can be easy to lose sight of what truly matters—helping people. Customers are inundated with options and are wary of traditional sales tactics. They want to work with salespeople who they can trust, listen to their needs, and provide valuable insights and advice.

This book is a guide for anyone who wants to become a *Blue Ocean Advisor*, a trusted advisor who stands out in a crowded market. A trusted advisor committed to removing their tools and products from the focus of their thinking and replacing them with their clients' most important goals. It provides practical strategies for building relationships, developing trust, and providing value to customers in a way that ultimately drives sales. Through real-world examples and case studies, readers will learn how to adopt the mindset of a trusted advisor and build long-lasting relationships with their clients.

In a world where the transactional salesperson is becoming increasingly irrelevant, the *Blue Ocean Advisor* is poised to become the salesperson of the future. This book will provide the tools and insights needed to succeed in the ever-changing world of sales and become a trusted advisor who consistently delivers results.

Whether you are just starting out in sales or are a seasoned professional looking to take your game to the next level, this book is for you. By following the simple path laid out in these pages, you will be able to build a massive book of business that is not only successful but fulfilling. You will be able to help people achieve their goals, and in doing so, you will achieve yours.

CHAPTER ONE

Why Doesn't Every Producer Have A Million-Dollar Book Of Business?

Our firm has worked with thousands of producers over the last 20+ years. Our goal is always to help a producer accomplish whatever his or her wildest dreams are from this business, and it's interesting to see some people respond with motivation and creativity to reach their goals while others seem to just get stuck.

Everyone that works with our firm knows that our favorite book is *The Obstacle is the Way* by Ryan Holiday. The whole idea behind the book is that action advances action. We live in America. We've got it made. Some may say we are soft.

Why do I say that? Because when you have it really good, what happens is, when you run into an obstacle, you tend to shrink from the obstacle. But know this, every producer reading this book can make $400,000 or $500,000 a year within three to ten years of getting into the business.

Why do we know that? Because we've seen it so often. Why is it that a lot of people aren't making that kind of money? Why is it that a lot of people don't have million-dollar or higher books? We have actually been studying this for many years.

We have been working inside agencies and alongside producers for over 20 years, and what we've learned is there are five reasons that not all producers have million-dollar books or higher. When you hear about these people with a $5 million revenue book or a $10 million revenue book, they're specialists at breaking through these obstacles. If you practice what we teach you in this book, you can break through each one of these barriers. We'll list them briefly, and then we will break each of them down for you.

We will discuss in this book practical applications to blow up every one of these obstacles so that when you're done, you will know that the impediment to action does advance action and that "the obstacle is the way," to quote Ryan Holiday.

The five obstacles/bottlenecks that we're all trying to continue to break through are:

1. *Expectations or vision* — Low expectations or a lack of real vision for my future.

2. *Time* — "If I just had more time."

3. *Who do I call on?* — Very few producers have a meaningful list and don't really understand their ideal buyer.

4. *What do I say to get in front of them?* — Simply getting more people to call me back and then getting them to meet with me.

5. *What needs to happen to get hired?* — Are you in the **Blue Ocean** (authentically different) or **Red Ocean** (same as everyone else)?

Bottleneck number 1: Expectations/Vision

This is going to seem so obvious. People don't wake up with $4 million books of business. They have this vision for what it would look like to have that book of business. Let me give you an example of how critical this is for you to lay out how big of a book you want in ten years, where you need to be in three years to get there, and then what your one-year goals are.

A guy reached out to us, admitting to having some level of call reluctance when prospecting. We were impressed by his level of self-awareness and soon after arranged for him to take an assessment called SPQ Gold. If you know anything about SPQ Gold, you know that the premise is that we were not born with call reluctance; it's actually a learned behavior. And so if it's learned, it can be unlearned.

After taking the test, we went over the results with one of the test interpreters, and I'll always remember what it revealed. If we were to ask you where call reluctance comes from, your answer would most likely be "fear of rejection" or something similar.

His number one reason for call reluctance was he had no long-term vision or goals for his business. The person that proctors the exam let us know a truth for most producers—nobody wants to prospect. Prospecting is something you have to do, similar to athletes not wanting to go to two-a-days, but that is what they have to do. They don't want to go to practice every day, but they want to play under the Friday night lights, and they want to play in Super Bowls. The bottom line is if we don't get this vision right, we will never reach our full potential or ever enjoy this business as much as we could.

Almost everything else about this book is going to be about your prospects and how to help them. This vision component is deeply personal. What do you want out of this business? Where do you want to be in three years and then ten years? Understanding those things will help define your one-year revenue goal.

Share your personal vision with your significant other and other important people in your life, including your mentors and close friends. Every decision we make should be filtered through the lens of where we want to be.

Sales and prospecting can be very difficult, and we get beat up frequently—we expect it. We're not going to shrink from it. We're going to run toward it, not away from it. Why? Our vision propels us forward despite the obstacle. This whole book could be about vision, but we know you've got to have your expectations and vision right, or nothing else matters.

In summary, a powerful vision for your future is the fuel in your furnace of desire. If you really want to get it right, don't think about your future in terms of what you think you can do but what you really want out of life and your business.

Bottleneck number 2: Time

The next bottleneck people run into is thinking they've run out of time. The truth is that we would have never seen $5, $10, $15, or $20 million revenue books of business if time were actually the problem. Time isn't the problem. The problem really goes back to the lack of vision. With the correct vision, we can continue to look for a way around or through the obstacle to continue to grow our books.

Everybody gets busy in this business. It becomes really simple. How do you get to be so busy? The primary reasons we routinely see are:

1. Too many accounts.
2. Too much service work and/or not delegating lower-level tasks.

We know that the Pareto Principle is a very simple way to blow up the time bottleneck. You may know the Pareto Principle by its more common name, the 80/20 rule. The 80/20 rule simply highlights that 80% of your revenue comes from 20% of your accounts, and the inverse is also true, that 80% of your accounts are generating 20% of your revenue.

Many years ago, we had an engagement in Southern California. We mention this one because it was a glaringly obvious example of the power of understanding the impact of the Pareto Principle.

The new client was a $5 million revenue agency. Before we could get to the conversation about growth, which was why they hired us, they told us they had a bigger problem. They let us know that they did not feel like they had any capacity to grow. That seemed like a funny thing to be sharing since they had already paid us to help them ramp up organic growth.

They shared that all of their service people were overwhelmed serving their clients. Recognizing that this was an agency of roughly $5 million in revenue, we asked them to take their largest 1,000 customers and their smallest 1,000 customers and tell us how much of their revenue was being driven in each. We asked them to pretend they could put all their 1,000 largest customers in one file cabinet and the 1,000 of their smallest customers in the other.

We then asked them how much revenue was in each file cabinet. It was eye-opening. Their top 1,000 customers generated $4,750,000. Their smallest 1,000 customers in the other file cabinet only generated $250,000. Again, the smallest half was only $250,000 in revenue, and the largest was just short of $5 million.

They sold those accounts to a friendly competitor later that day.

We asked them why they sold that book. We could have done other things with those accounts. Their answer was very revealing. They said that every day their employees walk in those two front doors (they pointed at them), and "there is only one way we know of that our employees will no longer work on accounts that are so small that a thousand of them only generate $250,000 in revenue, and that is to get rid of those accounts."

Maybe we remember this so vividly because they sold the book of business before we ever left. That's understanding the obstacle and executing the way to overcome it quickly!

This might seem like a stretch, but when people tell us they have a time problem, we believe they have a vision problem.

What do we mean by that? You can find every excuse for why you can't figure out what to do with a small customer that really shouldn't be in your book of business anymore. We know they are a cancer to growth at the producer and enterprise levels.

If your vision is strong enough and you want that multi-million-dollar book because of what it will do for you and your family, you will figure out a way to get those small accounts out of it. The Pareto Principle makes it a practical reality, but without a crystal-clear vision, most people won't leverage it.

Bottleneck number 3: "Who do I call on?"

When we were younger, we can both remember our mom talking about making dinner, which she did almost every night.

She would say, "I don't really mind making dinner. It's coming up with what I'm going to make that is difficult." I think that is very much like Bottleneck number three: "Who do I call on?" How does that bottleneck show up? Your prospect list is old or tired.

You may or may not know that you can build a fantastic prospect list off Sales Navigator within LinkedIn. We will talk later in the book about running the R.O.O.T.A. (Referral Out of Thin Air). We believe a salesperson not having LinkedIn Sales Navigator is akin to a carpenter not having a hammer. There is MiEdge and other free and paid sites to build prospect lists as well.

The main thing we really want to introduce here is that we've worked with some fabulous producers with multimillion-dollar books that take this very seriously and EVERY Friday at 9:00 a.m., without fail, tend to their list. They care for it like a master gardener tending to their prize rose bushes.

A simple tip for building a great list is to pick a vertical or two. By shrinking your world, it becomes easier to create a more meaningful list. Also, make sure you are adding the person that you want to meet or get in front of, not just the company name. We are in the people business, not the company business.

Now it's time for a really good story that we can tell around the first three bottlenecks. This is a story about a young man who we met around 2010. He had been in the business for just under three years, had roughly a $350,000 revenue book, and he wanted to grow immediately. When we got to know this guy, we realized that he had very high expectations for the future. That gets people like us excited because we know people who are motivated to do something special for themselves will do much better than those who are trying to live up to a sales manager's expectations. He had an event in his life that created an important reason for him to need to basically double his book in one year. In our early conversations, we wanted to understand how many accounts he felt confident he could write, and he said he could probably write ten accounts this year.

In his first year, he had written 12, but he called on anybody that would let him fog up their glasses to achieve that. He felt he could write ten accounts partly because there were a few holdovers from previous years he could possibly write in the near future. We asked him what his average account size was; it was $20,000 in revenue, and he wanted to write $400,000 this year. The math was pretty simple. He had to double his average account size if he wanted to reach this goal of $400,000 in revenue in a single year. One of the tweaks we made was that we took him from his average account size of $20,000 to $40,000, which became very important for him to be able to achieve his goal. Another thing we did was start to discuss who he needed to be calling on, not just the size of the account, but who to reach out to inside of the business. When we noticed his closing ratio was lower than it should have been, we realized that he was calling on somebody inside a business who could not tell him yes. We then switched the buyer, the type of person that he was calling on, from an HR person to a CFO. Our goal wasn't to alienate HR but to start looping in someone higher on the food chain.

Immediately, his results started to get much, much better. He not only hit that $400,000 revenue goal about four months in, he surpassed it. Since then, he has gone on to build a multi-million-dollar book, and this all started because he had really high expectations. We tweaked the type of business he was going after in terms of their size and who the buyer type was on the inside, which radically transformed how he approached the first three bottlenecks. The exercises we put him through really pushed him to think differently, and his ultimate vision coming out of that year was to have a $5 million revenue book by the time he was 40. He would have achieved his goals without us, but we are fortunate we got to help him shortcut that process potentially by many years.

Bottleneck Number 4: "What do I say or do to get in front of a decision-maker?"

Our number one coaching request would be to understand what to say to a buyer when we finally get one on the phone. *What do I say to get them to be more likely to meet with me?* We're going to actually move you a little further back in the continuum of getting in front of a new opportunity and look at a very different metric. People always want to focus on the conversation to appointment metric, which we do agree is very important.

But in 20 years of working with producers, studying seasoned producers, and thousands of new producers that our clients have hired, we've realized there's a different metric that we're going to ask you to focus on. It's a huge bottleneck to growth, and it is this: the attempts to conversation. This is simply how many dials it takes to get someone to call you back or get put through by the gatekeeper. We're going to show you how to take that from a 20 to 1 metric to a 5 to 1 metric or better and start getting into conversations with a lot more people.

We're also going to tweak the things that we would recommend that you talk about on a prospecting call. So many producers say the exact same thing instead of actually talking about something different. And we get it because, in the world that you are in, many of your tools and resources are the same. And so that kind of dictates what you're going to talk about. We're going to adjust that a little bit later in the book for you to really feel confident. First of all, we will help you to drastically improve your metrics from attempts to conversations and then with your conversation to appointment metric so that you feel like you will get a better result for your effort. You're going to get a much better result for the amount of time you spend. This bottleneck is the one that we get the most requests for help to overcome, and that's because it is the most difficult one. We believe one reason it is so much harder to prospect as an insurance advisor compared to a traditional salesperson is because of the strength of some of these incumbent relationships.

For every account we're going after, there's somebody on the other side of it that wants to keep it because they're being paid a renewal on it. Again, it makes it exponentially more difficult. As you already likely know, some of the most common reasons that you're not going to get in front of an opportunity is that a prospect is going to say to you, "I'm happy with my current broker," or "I don't have time for that right now," or "I'm all set," or "I'm not looking at that this year." They're treating you as a transaction or a commodity because you are in the red ocean. We're going to try to change the conversation for you to overcome these common objections. Even better, let's take the bat out of their hands before they even swing it.

Bottleneck number 5: What needs to happen to get hired?

Once we actually get in front of a prospect for the first time, what happens in that meeting is going to determine the path we take moving forward. Will it be their transactional process that throws you into the red ocean where you look and sound just like everyone else, or will you be able to lay out a better path that is different from their normal process that turns you into a commodity?

They want this to be transactional. They're trying to define us in a certain way and it limits the impact that we can have on their business. This is not on purpose; they're just used to buying insurance a certain way. They want us to follow their process because it's just the way they have always done it. Sadly, it doesn't help them, or us, to follow their process, and it is our job to introduce a better one, which, if they follow it, will generate a better set of outcomes for them and likely for us as well.

Let us give you an example of a client that transitioned to this different way of thinking where the quote/bid was not something she did on every deal. She said, "Look, I close 30% of the deals I work on, and it takes about 40 hours to get all the spreadsheets done. Everything that we do in a deal takes about 40 hours, and we close 30% of them."

Fast-forward one year. When she went to the method we will share with you in this book, she went from 30% closing ratios to 70-80%. And the time it took to get the deal closed was six hours instead of 40 hours, and she used a broker of record letter.

By the end of this book, you will learn how to lead to your tools, not with your tools. We will be doing things in their proper order, and the focus is going to be on your prospect, not you and all your stuff. We will take you out of the middle of your presentation and put them in the middle.

We want you to understand that the Holy Grail in sales is for you to get real buyers to be open and honest with you about their situation and what they want to see happen. If we do this correctly, we will not only write the account, but we will write it quicker and, in many cases, not have to give everything away to do it.

In short, we want you to be preoccupied with what you want to know about them, not what you want them to know about you.

CHAPTER TWO

The Foundation And Fundamentals Of Becoming A Trusted, Successful Advisor

As we worked side by side with salespeople our whole careers, we have this really unique vantage point where we get to meet people who just do it differently than others. It's really exciting when that happens. We don't believe we are gurus. We believe we're interested in studying this and getting our Ph.D. in sales and prospecting, and we study the gurus and great salespeople.

We read the books, and we have coaches ourselves that we believe make us better. We're going to get really tactical as the book advances, but for now, we would be making a big mistake if we didn't share with you the fundamental principles that the Blueprint rests upon. If you don't understand these, you'll probably struggle tactically with how we do something later in the book or the "why" behind how we might do something. We want to begin with a concept that we call "The Two Pitfalls" that all salespeople deal with and typically aren't very effective at overcoming.

We believe that, as insurance advisors, it's an even bigger problem than most salespeople outside of the industry have to endure because of the really strong incumbent relationships that your prospects have.

Let's discuss Sales Pitfall Number One.

Sales Pitfall number one is that <u>our prospects believe that we will say anything or do anything to win their business</u>. If you think about it, if prospects believed everything we said as salespeople, this would be a really easy job. We could make a lot of money if people always believed everything we told them.

They don't believe it for good reason. We've all been buyers. When a salesperson says something that is self-serving, we can sense that everything that comes out of their mouth will be to their benefit, and we have to deal with that.

This idea that prospects believe that salespeople will say anything or do anything to win their business is a huge issue. This may seem like a simple thing, but even when we show up to a meeting and we thank a prospect for spending time with us, we automatically begin to subordinate ourselves to them, and we give cues or hints that their time is more valuable than ours. Now, I'm not saying that to be rude by any stretch of the imagination. I would just be careful thanking people for their time. First, it does subordinate us, and secondly, (I see this all the time riding with producers for 15 years) they just show up as different people in a prospect meeting than they are normally.

It's this really flowery kind of church greeter kind of mentality that we see that creates a problem. It actually causes a buyer's resistance to go up instead of bringing it down. In fact, we were riding with a producer six or seven years ago, and he was highly technically trained. He came from the insurance company side. He was very well-liked by everyone that knew him.

For some reason, he could not win a deal. His agency leadership reached out to us and said, "We want you to come ride with him to see if there's anything that jumps out at you." So we hopped in the car with him and went to an appointment. We quickly realized that this guy's problem was that he had become very different from the one we all knew and loved. Once he got live in front of a new prospect, we think the best way to describe it would be he came across like a church greeter, and it was bothersome. It was so over the top.

We thought we needed to go to a nursing home and let him go room to room. They would love that personality there. It's not coming across very well on a sales call, though. We remember one of the comments he said was, "First of all, Mr. And Mrs. Prospect, we're honored that you would meet with us." We remember thinking, *Wow, that is really turning it on thick*. The fact that he said he was "honored" that they would meet with him. Real people don't do this in real life, and he didn't normally act this way either, and it was hurting him.

On a humorous note, we did find out after that sales call on the way back to the office that the salesperson was, in fact, a greeter at his church.

We think we are helping ourselves, but the opposite is achieved; it actually hurts us. We would rather you just be yourself and say something simple when you're going to meet a prospect for the first time. "Hey, I've been looking forward to the meeting." Or "It's nice to put a face with the name."

The more effective we are at eliminating sales pitfall number one, the better off we will be, and we do it by introducing ideas that lower buyers' resistance, not raise it. It could be something simple like, "We don't know if it makes sense for us to do business together moving forward, but we're here to see if there's a fit and see if there are any opportunities to work together."

That neutral type of language is automatically going to set you up better to avoid falling victim to pitfall number one as opposed to being overly nice, lighting the sparklers with a presentation that is like everyone else's: too salesy or overly grateful for the opportunity.

Be more neutral when you're meeting with the prospect for the first time by being preoccupied with what you want to know about them, not what you want them to know about you. *Let me repeat that.* Be preoccupied with what you want to know about them, not what you want them to know about you. If you bring some "give a damn" to the table and take an interest in them right out of the gate, they will sense that about you, and they will open up to you. They will tell you what you need to know to help them and be able to create value for them—AND FOR YOU.

Let's discuss Sales Pitfall Number Two.

Sales pitfall number two is that <u>our prospects decide our value before they ever really know it</u>. That comes into play probably more in the prospecting phase than at any other time in the sales continuum because we have this desire to tell them what we do, and then they think/say, "Oh, I have one of you already, and I really like them" or "I'm not going to meet with you because I don't have to because I know what you do"… BUT they really don't know what you do. We create this effect by the way that we approach initially, by leading with "I'm a broker," which is the most fortified position you could approach them with. We don't use these exact words, but to the prospect, it sounds something like this, "I want to be your broker. I know you have a broker, but I'm better than your broker."

This produces an automatic rejection most of the time. Again, it's why we call it the most fortified position. We will discuss later how to use curiosity and reciprocity to get into many more conversations with prospects than traditional methods.

Let's discuss another foundational concept known as the "Change Formula."

The Change formula was documented and simplified by a person named David Gleicher. If you would like to Google Gleicher's formula for change, you will be able to find out more about it and see its origins. This was not introduced to us as a concept that would impact our ability to be more effective salespeople, but we knew intuitively when we saw The Change Formula that it would have an impact on writing more business.

Here's how the formula reads: D multiplied by V multiplied by F is greater than R (DxVxF>R). The D stands for dissatisfaction, the V stands for vision for the future, and the F stands for first concrete steps. The R stands for resistance to change.

Like an algebraic equation, any of the variables on the left have an assigned value of zero to ten. Our goal is to have close to ten on each of these variables by the time we are at the proposal stage. If any of these variables is zero, then we will not have enough to overcome their resistance to change. Here's what The Change Formula is trying to tell us. If someone is going to overcome their resistance to change, there are three variables on the left side of the equation that are necessary for them to be able to do that, and each needs an assigned value. They have to be dissatisfied, have a powerful vision for the future, and first concrete steps that are not too complicated.

The first variable on the left side of the equation is dissatisfaction. What we mean is that a prospect has to be dissatisfied with their current situation if they are going to "change." As a salesperson, I have to understand if a prospect is not going to quickly admit to me where they're dissatisfied in their current situation, then my job is to create it. A typical producer may ask somebody, "Are you happy with your current broker?" Or "Are you happy with your current insurance program?" That's the producer's way of trying to figure out whether the prospect is dissatisfied with their current situation. In most cases, they're not dissatisfied, or at least early on, they are not willing to admit they are, so it becomes almost a worthless question. The prospect may tell us that they are unhappy because they want to get a quote/bid from us, and they have to be able to tell us they are unhappy or that "they aren't married to their broker" so they can get what they want. That way, we'll go ahead and give our quote/bid, even though their intention is never to hire us. As we move forward in this book, we will discuss how to effectively get a dissatisfied prospect.

Within The Change Formula, variable number two of the left side of the equation is vision for the future. We love to look ahead two years with a prospect and just simply learn from them, if all things were possible, what they would like to see happen over the next two years. What outcomes would they like to see come to pass that aren't happening right now?

Often, a really good vision casting session with the prospect can create a lot of dissatisfaction. Maybe they weren't that dissatisfied when the conversation started, but when they start telling us what they would really like to see happen, they get excited about the future and automatically become more dissatisfied with what is going on now.

Another great thing about casting vision with a prospect is when we do that, we get attached to that vision. They know that we can help them get there, and they see us as a part of the vision we just helped them create.

Part of our role as an advisor is to know what's possible. It's not only what they answer for us when we ask them about the vision question, it's also based on our wisdom and understanding to help them know what's possible. *Have you considered this outcome before?* More often than not, they say, "No, we haven't. We didn't know someone like you could help us do that." So, vision casting becomes this really important piece. In fact, within the Blueprint model, we would never give someone a proposal that we didn't understand what their two or three-year vision was about. What opportunities did they want to pursue that they weren't experiencing right now?

We would not give a proposal without that question being answered. We would also not give a proposal to a prospect without understanding where they were dissatisfied in their current situation. It could be a simple thing that we start with a vision and then ask them what roadblocks could keep that vision from happening, and that may be where their dissatisfaction is at its highest point.

We are very positive people around Blueprint headquarters. It would be hard for us to admit something we might be "dissatisfied" about, but we are more likely to admit something that we wish was different or something that we're frustrated with. There are different words we can use to get people talking, and we will continue to unpack those as we progress in the book. Hopefully, we can begin to see documenting where a prospect is dissatisfied, and their vision for the future are two really important pieces to us closing more business.

As stated earlier, the third component is "first concrete steps." Often, when producers present a proposal, there can be many tools and moving parts in a work comp program or an employee benefits program, etc. If we're not careful, it can be seen as too difficult, and the prospect might say, "This has been great, and you've given us a lot to think about." That is obviously not a good response, and we will show you how to deal with a proposal with many tools and capabilities you are bringing to the table. We will show you how to simplify your proposal and keep the focus on the outcomes instead of the "stuff," especially at the close.

If you will embrace The Change Formula, it is the closest thing to sales magic that we can come up with to help people understand all the boxes they need to check to be able to win a piece of business. It's always on our minds as salespeople when we are riding with producers. We once went on a sales call with a young producer, and it was about a 600-life group. We were meeting with the CFO. She was very sharp, and we knew right away that she was smarter than us and wouldn't be "sold" anything. A few minutes into the meeting, we asked her, like we do in the early moments of any sales call, "Is there anything that you want to make sure that we discuss? Let's begin there so we don't run out of time — ultimately, this is about you, not us. We have some things that are important to us, that we think matter, but we want to start with what you want to talk about."

Her response was, "I've been working with my current broker for nine years, and for the first six years, they were amazing, but for the last three years, they have not been hitting the bullseye."

A really funny part of this story to us is in that moment, the young producer I was with (because often our instincts are bad and the two pitfalls of salespeople came into play) responded with, "You don't have to worry about that with us, we know how to hit the bullseye. We're known for it (Blah, blah, blah)." We were able to redirect the conversation, but only because The Change Formula was on our minds. I asked her, "Can you tell us what your bullseye is?" Interestingly, she did not give us her bullseye. What she started doing instead was talking about all the different ways that she was dissatisfied with her current broker. From there, it was very easy for us to transition into another meeting to really unpack these issues in a deeper way. It was super simple to be able to document where she was dissatisfied. In the next meeting, we jumped into her vision for the future, and it made the process so much easier for us to be able to showcase our tools and resources through the backdrop of her very own formula for change that she gave us.

Continuing on with the fundamentals of being a *Blue Ocean Advisor*, let's look at how to effectively differentiate yourself from others.

It's easy to differentiate when we're comparing (as opposed to pitching). Maybe the only way to really differentiate is by comparing one thing to something else. It is difficult to differentiate between your tools and your ideas because we're just talking to prospects about how great a tool is or how great a resource is, how great our service team is, or whatever it may be that we find ourselves talking about all the time. We all know the feeling when we pitch that way when we look at our prospect and their eyes gloss over. It is difficult to differentiate while we're turning on a laser light show or when we're talking about the same things that other brokers talk about too.

Sadly, even people not in this industry use similar PowerPoints that are not that different from yours. The PowerPoint basically says, *We're amazing, and here's why you should hire us.* Whether it's a landscaper, a contractor, or an accountant, it doesn't matter. All these PowerPoints are the same. It is very difficult to differentiate when we are swimming in the red ocean, looking and sounding like everyone else, bloodying each other up over price.

In this book, we are proposing you approach this a different way than pitching and quoting. Instead of leading with tools and capabilities and carriers and market pressure, lead with a set of outcomes the prospect should be getting that we know they aren't getting (think of it as a comparison of outcomes instead of a comparison of stuff).

If we do this effectively, we aren't so vulnerable to everything getting funneled back through the incumbent for them to get the last look and be able to meet it or beat our proposal. So many producers have been run out of this business because they followed that model. That's why we're trying to set up a different way to differentiate. As Sandler Training disciples, we learned many years ago that when it comes to differentiation, <u>nothing is good or bad, better or worse, except by comparison.</u>

We have to be able to compare what's possible (vision) against how they're currently doing things. When we do that effectively, then we are differentiating effectively.

We mentioned earlier that it's difficult to differentiate in the tools and ideas realm. Surely you have heard the phrase "Ideas are a dime a dozen," and we have seen how everybody's PowerPoints are the same. So where we differentiate every single time is the execution layer, the results layer, otherwise known as the "outcomes" layer.

A prospect is much more likely to admit they're not getting an outcome than they are to admit to needing to use a certain tool that you might find valuable. When we talk about differentiation, we've got to get down into the "outcome" layer. If you don't agree with us on this premise, then it will be difficult for you to embrace how we navigate the process that we will discuss in later chapters.

We would commonly say to a prospect, "Tell me about the financial process you use to evaluate your insurance spend. How do you know that you're getting the best deal possible with that process? What are you comparing that to?" So, when we get down into that layer of execution, it's impossible for them to make up a process they don't have. Regardless of the topic, we want them to "walk us through your process," which is so much more powerful than a typical open-ended question.

If you want to be different, talk about different things. Differentiation stems from this idea that nothing is good or bad, better or worse, except by comparison. Remember this concept. We don't lead *with* our tools; we lead *to* our tools.

Your tools are important; let's just make sure we insert them at the right time and place, and that will be later in the process. Your tools help achieve important outcomes, so let's discuss the outcomes first (something they likely aren't getting), then let's discuss the tools inside of our execution process that gets to the outcome. We will have more on this in later chapters of the book.

We have looked at many different tools that brokers use over the last 20 years. We have noticed that there are only six or seven outcomes that all of them create, so let's talk about the outcome, and then the tool will become valuable later. If they don't want the outcome that the tool creates, they don't want the tool. We're much more likely to be able to get them to embrace our tools if we can first get them to embrace the problem that a tool solves or an outcome that they help create.

To continue the fundamental elements of being a *Blue Ocean Advisor,* let's discuss what we refer to as the Holy Grail in Sales.

Every guru we talk to or read or learn from personally would all teach the same thing, and I mean the best of the best. The true geniuses in the sales world would all tell us the same thing:

The holy grail in sales is getting real buyers open and honest with you about their current situation and what they would like to see happen.

If you want higher closing ratios, if you want to be meaningful to your prospects that will then become clients, if you want to get more referrals and all that comes with that, the holy grail in all of this is to get real buyers to be open and honest with us.

About what? Well, about what we need to know the answers to. This is such a crucial piece of this model we are unveiling to you. First of all, it needs to be a real buyer that can tell you yes, instead of just no. Information gatherers can tell us no but not tell us yes. If you want to improve performance and build wealth in this business, you must develop the skill of getting in front of and differentiating with real decision-makers.

If you take one thing out of this book and want your closing ratios to go up, you need to start calling on people who can tell you yes. So many salespeople and producers, especially in this industry, take someone through their sales process, create a proposal, and yet they don't win the deal. Sadly, it isn't because their process wasn't good. It was because they were calling on the wrong person. The person they dealt with could never tell them yes. They can only tell them no. It's a huge problem. It's a difficult problem to get solved without conscious effort.

Remember bottleneck #3 from chapter one was, "Who do I call on?" You've got to make sure it's somebody that's actually in the decision tree. Get that right and save yourself a lot of heartache. The second part of the holy grail in sales is to get them open and honest with you. We realized as young salespeople that if a prospect was not going to talk to us, if they weren't going to answer our questions, then they were not going to hire us. As we progress in the process of this book, we are going to give you many important questions to ask that are important for you to know. Equally as important: is your prospect willing to give you the answer? If they aren't, then that is valuable intel for you as you decide if this prospect has a good intent (remember their intent might be for us to get them a quote and not ever intend on hiring us). Not only do they need to talk to us, but they also need to tell us the truth. We're going to introduce you to some questions that we know they will not have a good answer for, and because they don't have a good answer, it's obvious to everyone they aren't performing as well as they could be.

Remember, we have to be able to get real buyers engaged. They have to open up to us even early in the conversation, especially once we get to phase two of the sales process, where it's all about them talking to us in a "discovery" type setting. Remember that the Blueprint process is built for prospects to open up to you with everything that you need to know to help them. As we move forward, we want to be preoccupied with what we want to know about them, not preoccupied with what we want them to know about us (that will come later).

Let's discuss another fundamental piece of being a *Blue Ocean Advisor,* and that is the "ideal client" way of thinking.

The ideal client model has changed our lives, as well as many others. Our coach and mentor, Curtis Verstraete of On Purpose IP, has spent countless hours helping us think through this over the years. You can also read about this in a book called *Book Yourself Solid,*" by Michael Port. When we go out for an initial appointment to meet with any prospect, there are all kinds of ways we've been taught to qualify a prospect. A simple part of our ideal client profile is we want to see if they will just talk to us and will they open up to us? There are many more pieces to the ideal client model, including how we market ourselves to attract the prospects that we want, but once we enter into dialogue with a prospect for the first time, that requires a different mindset and skillset. Their answering our questions is a simple criterion anyone can add to their ideal client profile immediately.

Another one, and maybe a bigger one, is: will they let us do our best work with them? Ultimately that will lead us to a process for a prospect to go through to get a better set of outcomes. Again, we will unpack this more in the book as we progress, and you will see how we tactically get a prospect to go through it with you. When they agree to it you are automatically put into a high closing ratio situation.

One of the biggest decisions a salesperson can make is to walk away from somebody that's not an ideal client, and that begins with, *Are they willing to answer your questions and tell you the truth?* Doing this will speed up your revenue growth and make you happier in the long run.

What we've learned is that if we only spend our time with ideal prospects and ideal clients, we love what we do much more. We feel affirmed, and we feel positive. We have the confidence level it takes to prospect daily.

In the ideal client model, your clients will also value you differently, and they will open up all of their relationships to you because you're different. They'll trust that they can do that for you. Yet, if we step outside of our value system on what an ideal client is, then that's when we get into trouble and won't like our job as much, and our clients won't like us as much.

Let's look at another fundamental attribute of a Blue Ocean advisor by contrasting the difference between a salesperson and an advisor.

In our careers, we have spent a lot of time trying to understand what an insurance salesperson or insurance advisor is all about. We heard this statement from our client, who said, "I want to be perceived as a trusted advisor." We thought, *Wow, what a great thing to want to be. Let's work toward that. Let everything we do point in that direction.*

Then we would go ride with producers that wanted to be seen and heard as trusted advisors, and we would walk away thinking that we were not exactly sure what an advisor does, but we have a feeling that what we just witnessed was not it. This information dump on how amazing I am and how amazing my firm is, for some reason, not what we had in mind when we heard from clients that they wanted to be seen as an advisor. We are fortunate to have worked with people that laugh alongside us as we figure things out.

We began researching and studying what an advisor really is. We had some clients that we really felt embodied the "advisor" title. We also met Curtis Verstraete of On Purpose IP. He was way ahead of us, and he had a model for an advisory process. It changed everything for us when we were able to see exactly what an advisor should be doing if they really are an advisor. We would always ask salespeople, trying to determine the difference between a salesperson and an advisor. In fact, in our workshops, a standard exercise is to get participants to give us adjectives to describe a salesperson, and we would get very common answers that you might expect—very self-focused-type answers. They're talkative, pushy, and they really are not concerned about what's in it for the buyer. They care about the commission they're trying to get and those types of descriptions. After asking participants to describe a salesperson, we asked them to describe an advisor. We heard very different answers, such as, "They care about their clients." "They're unbiased about what's in it for themselves." "They're objective, and they provide real solutions."

Now, again, one of the reasons that an advisor often can do that is because they have already been paid or at least that has been decided already. Whether it's an attorney or a doctor or a CPA or whomever, they're probably already being paid, or maybe even that's been discussed. They know what they're going to get paid, so they can be truly unbiased about the solution. Here is what we found; hopefully, you will find this good news. We can determine if they see us as a salesperson or as an advisor based on the same criteria. We're either going to be trusted, client-centric, objective and highly paid, or we're going to be self-centric and talk about our products and features, trying to close all the time with a focus on our commission. We're going to determine whether or not they see us as an advisor or as a salesperson. The primary takeaway that we want you all to be thinking about after having studied this for 20 years is if you want to be perceived as an advisor, the best way to get people to be open and honest with you and to tell you what's on their mind, is for you to be objective about what is in it for you or maybe even better, quit worrying about what's in it for you. On the other end, stop worrying about whether or not you get paid, and you will be much more likely to get paid.

The idea behind that is if you're going to serve a prospect out of their own need, they're going to let you do your best work with them, and you're going to come up with better solutions. The closing ratios go through the roof. The relationships that we have and the referrals that we get when we approach it this way become exponentially more important.

So again, it's not enough that we simply have this belief of being objective about what's in it for us that makes us an advisor. We know where to look to help people. For example, think about a doctor. If you went to the doctor, what would you do if they wheeled in a cart with a projector on it and had a PowerPoint about where they went to medical school and how much better their stethoscopes are than other doctors, and how their x-ray machines were better? Then they began to brag about how their nurses and service team were superior. What if they said, "Hey, at one time we were a really small firm, and now we're a part of 'Bigger and Better Broker' or we are members of 'A Bunch of Us Association,' and we picked up even better resources"? Just how odd would that be? As an industry, we do that all the time with our PowerPoints.

In another way, how odd would it be for a doctor to walk into the lobby and start guessing what people might need to be prescribed? Prescribing medication or treatments before an examination would lead to trouble. We may try to shove a capsule down somebody's throat of self-funding, or some piece of technology, a certain insurance company that we partner well with or whatever it may be. That is not the role of an advisor, and it's certainly not a Blue Ocean. We do that all the time in our world, but that is not the way an advisor operates, is it?

Keep in mind, as you move forward, that you must be objective about what's in it for you. You need to know where to look. You won't start the relationship talking about yourself like a salesperson would. Doctors take patients into an examination room and begin to understand their current situation, what kind of trouble they're having, and what they are struggling with. Only then do they start making recommendations. That is what advisors do. That's what the Blueprint process is going to enable you to do. Let's discuss a universal set of steps that all advisors follow. Whether you use these words or not doesn't matter, but all advisors follow an advisory process.

Step one is "discovery."
Step two is "planning."
Step three is "implementation."
Step four is "progress review."

You don't have to call each stage what we call it. "Discovery" could be "review" or "audit." You get the idea. These are just four words that we use to explain a universal set of steps that make up an advisory process — discovery, planning, implementation, and review.

So now that it's not enough that we have this process that you can follow, and you can look at Graphic 2.1 (below), a sample process that we would actually show a prospect. We ask them to go through this with us so that we can understand their situation better. We make it clear that we're going to be able to make recommendations once we understand their situation better, and we'll show them a set of tools that they likely haven't seen before to help them in their current situation achieve the vision that they are trying to work toward.

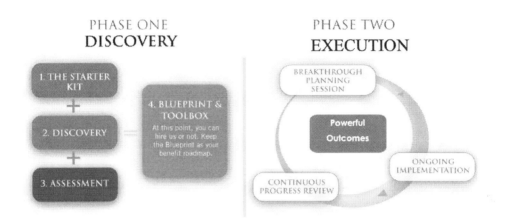

Graphic 2.1

There's a sample picture of it on Graphic 2.1, but it's not enough that we have an advisory process. Advisors don't veer from the process either. They don't start in the planning phase and then move back to the discovery phase later. That's how they get in real trouble. That's how mistakes are made. If you want to be perceived as an advisor, you need to start where advisors start, and that is some type of assessment, some type of review, or some type of discovery. Otherwise, you're skipping the most vital step of an advisory process. If a doctor skipped that, they would end up in prison. If an attorney skipped the discovery phase of what they do, they would never win a case. What we're proposing is that you start with discovery and work your way out from there. Discovery is the holy grail in sales.

We mentioned earlier in the book that differentiation is only found by comparing one thing to the next. And so most people reading this book really want to be different. If you were to show a prospect the graph we just showed you of what an advisory process looks like, it's the beginning of them seeing that you are different. They can compare that to most brokers that are offering a quote/bid as a way to differentiate. The real start for an advisor to differentiate is to show them an advisory process and what they can get from this different approach compared to what they receive with the typical industry-driven quote/bid.

CHAPTER THREE

The Initial Meeting: What Happens When We First Meet With A Prospect?

We started Blueprint in February 2005 based on one simple premise: *What if we could have a place to take a prospect that was any place other than a quote/bid? What if we gave them an alternative to a quote/bid as the first step that they would take with us?* Whether that was some type of review or analysis or whatever that may be. It was a chance to understand some things about them, and it was not a quote/bid. It was them talking to us, not us talking to them. If we could pull that off, we could end up weeding out those prospects that had no intention of hiring us.

It's interesting how prospects may think they're actually doing us a favor by letting us quote/bid their insurance. We realized early on, while riding with producers on sales calls, that these prospects thought they were doing us a favor by letting us quote/bid even though they didn't intend to hire us. It's as if we, as brokers, were going to get some kind of credits from insurance companies, like airline miles or something. We soon realized that if we didn't have a way to figure out a prospect's intentions, we could end up doing a lot of work and never have a real chance at winning a deal. Our company, Blueprint, was built on that premise first and foremost. Again, what if we had an alternative to the quoting process as a first step to take a prospect toward, and it gave us a lot of intel about what their real intentions were?

That first step with a prospect, we believe, should be more valuable than a quote/bid. We're not saying that we're never going to quote/bid; we're just saying we're not going to start there. In essence, the quote/bid is going to be the last financial lever that we will help them pull. So, that was the premise that Blueprint was built on, and it's really evolved from there. We have also realized over the years that closing ratios are as much impacted by who we end up having in the room with us as it is by the process we take people through or our conversations.

Salespeople can have a really good process. They can be great salespeople who ask the right questions, define the next steps and ask for the business, but it will be less effective if they don't have the right people in the room. Our data shows it's actually much less effective. As we discuss how we handle the initial meeting, it's very difficult in an initial meeting to get the right people in the room. We often don't, which is going to make that second meeting even more important to us as we progress in this conversation and explain why the Blueprint process is built the way that it is. In fact, if you look at the next graphic, there's a simple baseball diamond (which illustrates the point we are making).

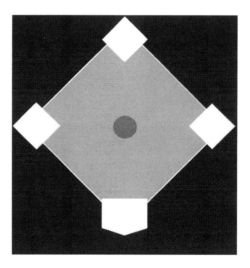

GRAPHIC 3.1

In its simplest form, the Blueprint process follows the same steps as a base path on a baseball field. First base represents an initial meeting. The initial meeting is intended to last around 20 to 30 minutes. They may go longer, but we are in the prospecting phase, so we ask for only 20 to 30 minutes for the initial appointment. It is intended to be a brief meeting to see if there's a fit, and we are hoping to get the prospect to agree to the next meeting (2nd base). Our goal would be to contrast our process to their process and how our process will deliver a different set of outcomes.

There is a bigger win for the prospect by going through our process instead of their process, which typically is some type of quote/bid or a request for proposal (RFP), where all of the focus is on us, the broker, instead of their company and their goals. We want to change that to bring the focus off of us, the broker, and onto the actual prospect. Let's focus on them, what they're trying to do, and the roadblocks that could impede progress. We need them to go through our process, and the initial meeting is set up to make sure the likelihood of that happening is as high as possible.

As you can see, represented by second base in the graphic, in our world, second base represents what we call a discovery meeting. Feel free to call that by a different name, but it is a very important phase of any sales process. It is what takes the focus off of us and puts it onto them. It is where we find out how to make our tools and capabilities relevant to their situation (value creation). That is a chance for us to really understand what the prospect is trying to do and give us a sense of what we could be doing differently to serve them better based on many different variables. Whether it's an employee benefits program or a risk management/insurance that we're looking at, it's important that we have a thorough discovery phase. We already made that case earlier in chapter two when we were discussing the importance of an advisory process, that it always begins with discovery. Again, in the Blueprint process, second base is that discovery meeting. It lasts 60-90 minutes and can go longer when they start talking.

Just like in baseball, when we get all the right stakeholders into the discovery meeting (second base), that is a scoring position. Our closing ratios are basically the same from second base as they are from third base. Third base represents a proposal, and we call it a "Blueprint," but our clients have many different names for it.

Now let's get more tactical on the initial meeting. This chapter is about getting a prospect to abandon their process and go through ours instead. We will walk through this in three different phases of the initial meeting – the open, the middle, and the third part, transitioning to Discovery (second base).

We recommend reading both approaches for Employee Benefits and Property and Casualty (P&C), even though they are very different. A savvy salesperson will pick up good ideas from both sides.

Employee Benefits:

The Open

Before we even get to the meeting, there should be a mindset shift toward them and the idea that we aren't going to "sell" them anything. Before we went into an initial or discovery meeting, one of our favorite people in the world would always make us bow our heads and pray. She did not pray that we would win the deal (like we probably would), she simply prayed that these people we were about to meet with would be better off when we left them than before we got there. Let us tell you, when she was in a meeting, people would open up to her like no one we have ever seen. It's because she cares about them and their success, and it just jumps out at everyone. She would never consider just pitching and selling and they knew it. The immediate trust and rapport she built because of her undying commitment for them to win was next level. It might not surprise you; she has built a phenomenal firm and reputation with a massive book. A simple way to get into the right mindset is just to take the approach that you're going to help them. It works every time. You will get them talking with that approach faster than any other, and anyone can do it with a little commitment to giving a damn. In fact, you can use this book to prop open the door if you get this concept. This thought process will help you create a dynamic that lowers buyers' resistance instead of raising it. Again, this is something we think about all the time.

Our instincts are not always right; they don't always serve us well. A lot of the things we say and do that we think create trust actually don't create trust. They create the opposite effect. They make a buyer's resistance go up. We have to have it low. They won't talk to us if we don't get this right.

Because our job is to really lower buyer's resistance, it is absolutely imperative that we do things and say things in order for them to sense that we're not there trying to sell them anything. A practical way to open up the discussion is to let the prospect know, "We don't come to these meetings assuming that it makes sense for us to do business together. We're here to see if there's a fit and if there are any opportunities that we can work on together, and if so, let's keep talking." They don't know we mean "keep talking" in a formal discovery meeting, but that's ok. They will as we "transition to discovery.".

We are trying to create this neutral environment where they see us as somebody who's not going to say anything or do anything to win their business (pitfall number one). It's powerful if you get good at it and you see your prospect relax.

Beyond lowering buyers' resistance and creating trust to get them talking, we ensure we check in on what they want to get out of the meeting. You will be shocked at how many people have something on their minds they are willing to share if we will let them. We can find out the main thing we need to solve for them by asking that question, and it needs to be standard operating procedure. If you are a sales leader reading this book, like me, I would add it to your list of questions to ask a producer when they come back from an initial meeting. "When you asked them what they wanted to get out of the meeting, exactly how did they respond?"

Within the initial meeting, it is important that we don't solve problems when they bring them up. We want to begin probing around the issue they brought up and see how real it is, how long it has gone on, and if they have tried to solve it already. It will be a great reason for them to go to second base with us if we solve the problem. It is always better when we can show patience there. It will keep us in advisor status and set us up for a proposal that creates value. When we can stack things up against the status quo (and the incumbent), it's always better than a one-off solution too early.

Instead of solving problems too early, we recommend planting some seeds of doubt that they're being taken care of as well as they could be and like they should be, as opposed to presenting a solution or a tool or a resource that we don't know if they need yet. Let's wait until third base. A key component to being a *Blue Ocean Advisor* is that we lead to our tools, not with our tools. We will get to solve their problems later, and in a big way, I promise.

Beyond planting seeds of doubt about their situation, it's also powerful to create curiosity about what's possible if they approach this the right way. Planting seeds of doubt and creating curiosity go hand-in-hand. We will discuss how to do that shortly.

The Middle

Once we have created the right environment with buyers' resistance low, we want to start asking them some questions and see if they will answer them. Remember, the Holy Grail in Sales is getting real buyers to be open and honest with us about their current situation and what they would like to see happen.

The graphic below is a sample of how we can get a buyer talking. It is a simple left/right column comparison that we refer to as The Performance

Spectrum (see Graphic 3.1). It's designed to compare and contrast how two different types of companies approach their employee healthcare. You can have some fun with this tool.

It's a great opportunity for us to check in with the buyer and ask them, "Hey, where would you put yourself on the spectrum?" And commonly, people will give themselves a middle-of-the-road score, and even more commonly, they will respond with, "Hey, some of these things we are really good at, and some we are not." But the point is, and we talked about this when we were talking about the components of differentiation, is that nothing is good or bad, better or worse, except by comparison. And this chart is a simple comparison for them to go, "Which side of this spectrum am I on?" If you are a sales leader, I would ask a producer, when coming back from an initial meeting, "When you walked them through the performance spectrum, how did each person rate their company's performance?" It will help drive important behaviors, especially for newer producers that don't have all of this figured out yet.

On the left side are those things that lesser-performing companies are dealing with compared to higher-performing companies. You can see on the left side, it's more reactive, it's not very transparent, and it's frustrating. The math doesn't make sense. Employees are not that enthusiastic about the benefits, which really impacts our return on investment. Because of that, HR is overly burdened and so it's just kind of a mess, or it can be a mess. Yet on the right side of the performance spectrum, it's very proactive. Our program is transparent. They understand why they're paying what they're paying. The financial levers they're pulling are crystal clear. They're not overpaying. And they have a way of comparing that to others, and they know it. Their employees are happy with the benefits that are being offered. HR is not overly burdened. They're actually working on corporate initiatives. Overall, they feel like for the money they're spending, it's really working for them.

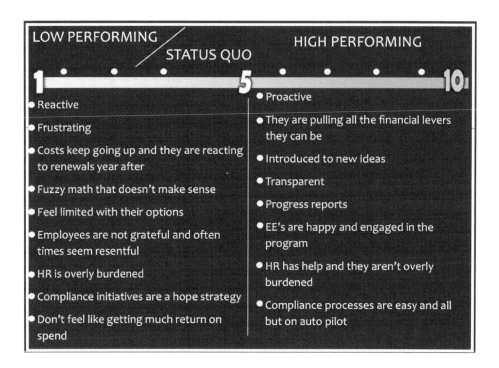

We just want to see if they're going to be open and honest with us about their current situation. And then again, I'm not going to drill down into those. If they say, "We're not doing that well, we give ourselves a five or a four or a six on the spectrum scoring." Or if they say, "We do well at some of these, not so well at others," I'm not going to probe into which ones are which. I'm just making the case that there are different outcomes for these people that approach it a certain way. And by the way, that way, it's going to be the *Blue Ocean Advisor* way. We know going in that we have a way to help them perform better. And that's what the setup to this is. So, we will ask a buyer, "We mentioned here that the high-performing companies know why they're paying what they're paying. They understand the financial levers that make a difference, and they're pulling them. Let me just ask you, Mr. And Mrs. Buyer, walk me through the process you have that gives you confidence that you're getting the best financial deal possible. And what are you comparing that to?" Again, we know they don't have a good answer for this; we just want them to admit it.

We've already lowered the buyers' resistance. They trust us. You know they don't have a good answer to that question. Notice that we asked them to walk us through a process. It's hard for them to make up a process they don't have on the fly. So we want them to walk us through a process that we know they don't have.

And if they do have a good answer to those questions, our potential to find out quickly whether we're going to move forward with these people increases dramatically. If they're already doing extremely well on all of this, we find out in 30 minutes instead of 30 hours' worth of bid/quoting whether we're going to move forward with these people. So, we love asking that question. It's one of our favorite questions to ask because it's a really quick check-in to find out if we have somebody who is willing to tell us the truth.

And again, what if they do have an amazing process for that? We might even learn something that we can use with every prospective client we encounter down the road. But typically, that question is going to get us where we need to go. That's going to be a soft spot in their armor that will allow us to set up the Blueprint process to get them to take that second meeting with us (scoring position) because, by the time we get to the end of the Blueprint process, they're going to have a better feel for all that they could do to get a better financial deal and know how to get the best deal.

And then also there are some good ROI questions that I like to ask in an initial meeting. So there are things that we can do to make sure they're getting the best financial deal. And then the other side of the coin is that there are things we can do to make sure they're multiplying the effectiveness of each employee benefit dollar they're spending.

Let us explain what we mean. As we look at high-performing programs, let's say we do find out that somebody is in the right financial structure. They're pulling all the financial levers that they can, and they're getting the best financial deal possible. But if their employees don't value it, it's not a high-performing program. It's not doing for them what they had hoped it would do. In fact, if you look at Graphic 3.2 (below), there has been all types of research over the years that clearly shows we can show a prospect this graphic and say, "Look, even above average plans, if there's not an effective communication and engagement strategy, only one in four people inside of the company will value it, sometimes spending millions of dollars a year."

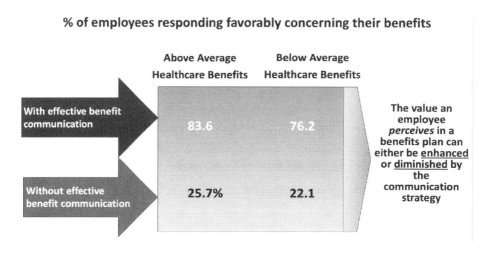

Graphic 3.2 Quadrant slide

"Companies are spending millions of dollars a year, and only one out of four people will value the benefits that are being offered. Yet, when you look at even a below-average plan, if there is an effective communication and engagement strategy, then closer to 80% of the people value it." So this is a really powerful concept.

Again, all we're trying to do is get them to go to the next phase of our process, which is the discovery phase. They've already admitted they don't have a good financial process. Now I'm going to get them to admit they don't have a really good process to impact how employees feel about the benefits that are being offered. And even an HR person will admit that employees don't appreciate all that they're doing for them. Those are two simple examples that have worked for us over the years to get a buyer curious about what these processes look like, to really plant some seeds of doubt that they may have seen everything they could see. And it's a powerful motivator to get them to spend 60 to 90 minutes with us in the discovery session, which we're going to explain in more detail in the next chapter, which is just a really simple, structured conversation to understand what situation could be different.

Transitioning to discovery

As we begin to try to close the initial meeting, get them to second base, the discovery meeting, we are going to say:

There are really four different outcomes that you're going to get by going through the process with us that would require you to spend about 60 to 90 minutes with us in the discovery session and then about another 60 minutes with us as we roll out what we would call a Blueprint. By spending this time with us, you will understand how your program compares to high-performing programs and what you could be doing differently to perform better.

Second, you're going to understand what financial levers you could be pulling that you're not aware of, and you're going to have a better sense of a financial process and a way to know that you're getting the best financial deal possible.

Thirdly, you're going to have a way to take the dollars that you're spending and multiply their effectiveness through a series of toolboxes that you can see here that we're going to be drawing from to help you fill up your toolbox to run this more effectively and get a better return.

And lastly, you're going to understand your team will be aligned around what you could be doing differently in a plan that we call a blueprint. And the blueprint is yours to keep whether you hire us or not.

We have worked with a mega-producer who is an absolute monster at writing business and also mentoring people. We would all be lucky to have someone like him to mentor us, and you would understand why if you heard the way people speak about him. He refers to the concept we discussed as "What, Why & ROI." He believes, and so do we, that every producer needs to know these three things—especially the ROI for someone if they will go through the process. If you know what is in it for them, and that reason is a good reason for them, they will do almost anything you ask. In short, most people don't want to go through a process, but they will endure the process if they get something meaningful out of it. You need to know what that is.

Often, saying "whether you hire us or not" makes producers feel uncomfortable because it's counterintuitive (Opposite George). What we have found, though, is that the Holy Grail in sales is getting real buyers open and honest with us. The process that we're outlining does that for you as a producer. And what you will find is that 7 to 8 out of 10 people hire you once the real buyers get in the room. In the discovery phase, it is a 70%-80% closing ratio. We're weeding out those people who really aren't trying to get it right but want you to give them a quote/bid because they need one or fill out an RFP because they need one when the deck is already stacked against you. Let's weed those people out. Let's get the people really looking to perform better to go through this process. They're going to get those four outcomes. And again, if our intent is good, and we're saying that it should be, and we talked about that in chapter one and chapter two, why it's important that our intentions are good.

If your intentions are good, people will take us up on this. And even if they're a little bit hesitant, we can say to them, "Hey, you're going to get these four outcomes whether you hire us or not. I'm curious, why won't you take me up on this?" We can gently press them a bit, and you can also probably tell that the Challenger Sale has greatly influenced what we believe and how we interface with the prospect. So our point is that if our intentions are good and we actually have a better way to help these people, then we can challenge their way of thinking differently than we can if we're just salespeople.

Property and Casualty:

We've laid out a baseball diamond. It's really cute when you go to a T-ball game and a five-year-old runs from first to third. Well, it's not cute in professional sales. And we see it all the time in the P&C world. We show up for the initial meeting, and we collect a stack of documents. We skip second base. That's the Holy Grail in sales, where we get those real buyers in a room and get them open and honest for their benefit to see what's possible with their insurance and risk management. So we skip second base, and like the little T-ball player, we go from first to third. And what do we do in between? We go to our markets. We collect all these documents on first base after the initial meeting. And then we take them to market.

Here's what's funny. They may have been with their broker for five or six years. You've spent a total of maybe two to three hours with them. No matter how good the quote/bid is that you have from your favorite carrier, it's not enough. They're not going to fire their broker. People make decisions emotionally and justify them logically. This is a huge emotional decision. It's not enough. And so think about this. This may have happened to you. You go out on the initial meeting. You gather documents. You submit those to the insurance carrier of choice. You get them back. You take your favorite one. You develop a proposal, and you take it out to your prospect, and you know you've done a fabulous job. You're saving them. They're spending $200k right now. Your proposal is at $160k. They told you in the initial meeting they would move. They told you they're not married to their broker. And so you give them their proposal, and they tell you, this looks really good. Check back with me on Friday. And then, when you check back Friday, you can't get them on the phone. You talk to them early the next week, and they say, "Hey, we're sorry. This was really good, but at the end of the day, there just wasn't enough reason to move." And you're confused about what happened, or maybe you know what happened. They called their broker (I honestly don't believe they called their broker trying to do something immoral to you). They called their broker because they like their broker, and their broker said something like this, "Mr. Client, if that proposal is real, you need to take it. But I've got my doubts. For somebody to save you that much money, I've got my doubts. Let me take a look." Lo and behold, they look. But in the meantime, they go back to their favorite incumbent carrier, and they get them to match your price at the end of the day because they own the relationship. They can sell that. You all know it's played out thousands of times.

We are convinced it's the reason why our industry has a 90% to 95% renewal retention. People are not calling the incumbent broker back, asking them to match the premium. They're calling them back because they feel guilty. They feel guilty they went out and got other quotes/bids. We don't know why that is; we just know that it is. And so what if you decided I'll never again go from first to third base? It could be the greatest thing you get out of reading this book. You don't even know what you'll talk about on second base yet. But you know I'm not going from first to third anymore.

We aren't going to go into this in depth, but a little bit of an idea. How can you get somebody that's really predisposed to want a quote/bid off that idea? They want you to go from first to third because that's what they've been taught. That's what we taught them. But we know that favors the incumbent, but more importantly, it hurts your prospect even more.

There's no way you can help somebody that you don't know. Really help them, anyway. We had an underwriter tell us once that they want to know if the producer that sent them the submission knows the owner of a company. They want to know that the company's owner actually cares about safety. And we're like, you may not know that, but you can't skip meeting the owner of the company. We've got to meet the person.

We've got to be able to tell their story. So let's talk about what a good initial meeting looks like on a commercial account. And it starts with this idea. You are not there to convince anybody of anything or manipulate anybody. Because here's the deal.

When you present them with new information that they didn't know about, how do they react to it? And you're going to work with those that react favorably. And I think that takes a lot of pressure off you. This will change your life in sales.

You're looking for ideal prospects. In the initial meeting, they will raise their hand and say to you, "I'm ideal." We learned this from Michael Port in his book, *Book Yourself Solid*. He does a beautiful job of explaining this. We're not going to ask the question in this way, but we're only going to go to second base or discovery. We're only going to move forward with people that will take us up on this one thing. This one thing we're not going to ask people, "Can you fire your broker?" That's too much too soon.

They don't know us, as we've already said. They're probably going to be forced to lie to us if they want us to give them a second bid just to keep their favorite incumbent broker honest. So instead of asking, "Can you fire your broker?" In our initial meeting, we're asking this simple question: "Will you let us show you our best work?" That's it. Very simple.

The sales process we've developed is designed in the initial meeting to show people what's flawed with the current system and how we built our best work to fix the flaws. If you look at Graphic 3.3, we call this "market mayhem." We start out with initial meetings, something like this. "We've really been looking forward to this meeting." Notice I didn't say thank you for taking the time to meet with us.

Our youngest brother Brian played football at LSU, and he talks about protecting your half of the field. Brian says if you've ever seen a fight take place before a college football game with a bunch of 19-year-olds pumped up with testosterone, maybe it's Alabama vs. Auburn, Michigan vs. Ohio State, or Texas vs. Oklahoma. These guys have hated each other forever. That's in their DNA. And he says, when you see those fights, what happened was somebody was coming over to the other person's half of the field during warmups.

And he says sales is no different, that we give up too much of our field. Buyers want to respect us. They want us to be advisors, not peddlers. But we go in, and we pin ourselves back on our own 40-yard line by saying things like, "Wow, thanks for agreeing to meet with us." We rode with a producer once who opened the meeting with, "We are honored that you would meet with us."

Now think about the position that automatically puts you in, subordinating you. They're going to do everything they can to subordinate you. You don't need to help them. So let's change our language to – "I've really been looking forward to this meeting. I've heard nice things about you." And as we look to lower sales resistance and make them not hate that they're in this meeting, we'd say, "Hey, look, we haven't forgotten we asked you for 20 minutes. We're not going to be here any longer than that unless you are asking a lot of questions. We've only got 30 minutes anyway. By the way, we're not going to ask to quote/bid your insurance; I mentioned that on the phone. We recognize you've got relationships. We're long-term players. We're playing a long game here but have a simple agenda. We want to walk you through what we mentioned on the phone. But before we do that, is there anything you want to ensure we cover? Because we want to make sure it's a good use of your time."

We are so focused on the idea that they know this is all about them, for their sake. We're not talking about us, how big we are, how great we are, how many employees we have, or how many tools we have. We're asking them, "Have you got anything you want to discuss? We'll throw our agenda away. We called you, so we came with the agenda. That's why you took the meeting.

But we can throw it in the trash. What do you want to talk about?" We ask that question for two reasons. A, to show them it's about them, but B, to see if they have some pain that they want to tell us about. We won't ask, "Do you have any problems with your current broker?" That's usually a throwaway question.

"I'm not married to them," they might say.

They have to tell you what you want to hear for them to get what they want (the 3rd bid). That's not our model. We feel like that's a little more peddler language, but we can say, "Hey, if there's anything you want to talk about, we do want to make sure that we cover that today." If they say no, then we're going to go to Graphic 3.3, which we call "market mayhem."

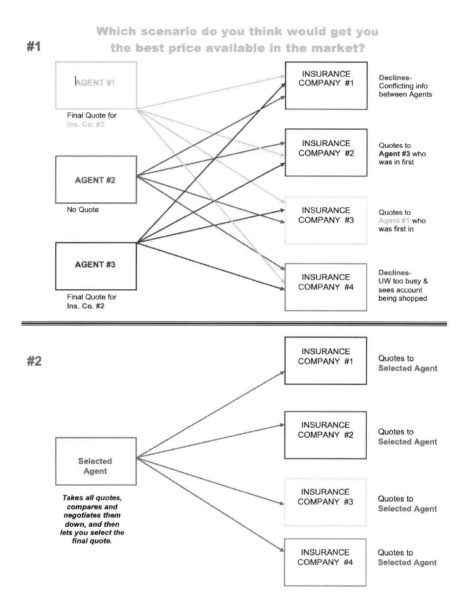

Graphic 3.3 "Market mayhem"

And here you're going to challenge the status quo. If the quote/bid process yields 90% wind of the incumbent, as evidenced by 90% renewal retention year over year in our industry, why would you play that game, especially if it's bad for them? So you're going to show them how that game works. We've got three brokers going to four different carriers. You can see that markets are being blocked.

When we talk about challenging the status quo, it doesn't have to be done in an obnoxious way.

We want to share an interesting story. A couple of years ago, we had a young man that went out to see a lady at the initial meeting. And here are the rules that she gave him:

> "We're an 8/14 renewal. All quotes/bids have to be in by August 1 (By the way, this was in early June). We do not assign markets. If you and a broker get into an argument over a market, we won't do a broker of record to give it back. There's no broker of records. Those are the rules."

Now, I think as a young salesperson, my response would have been, "Okey doke." As an older salesperson, I probably would have told her where to go, and it wouldn't be polite. But listen how he challenged the status quo. She was in the middle of "market mayhem," and he very politely said, "Hey, that's one way to go about it, and I think I know why you're doing it. May I show you a different way?" He laid out our initial meeting. Just like I've discussed, he invited her to a discovery meeting. When we heard about the story, it was two to three days after the discovery meeting when this lady made him and my client her broker through a broker of record letter. Think about it. She had set up the worst possible process. But you know what? She actually turned out to be an ideal prospect. When we showed her a better way in a different way, we didn't manipulate her because we couldn't. We didn't convince her of anything. We laid out logically and empirically why it's better to look at this thing through the risk manager route, not the broker route. She actually agreed with us. Nobody had ever laid that out in a way that made sense. So I hope that really brings everything together inside of the initial meeting. You remember how this young producer approached that, and we try to replicate it when we can.

When market mayhem is in play, carriers are declining the risk because it's got different information. One carrier declines the risk because they know it's over-shopped. You tell the prospect what you think is wrong with this, but you're on such good footing. Based on *The Challenger Sale: Taking Control of the Customer Conversation*, the preeminent book after the crash of 2008, you're on solid ground when you're challenging an old, antiquated, tired buying model.

So here you talk about what you think. Some people think you're letting the market pick the broker. People say, "Hey, you're literally letting the incumbent broker block all the markets when they get that request for loss runs in an attempt to create competition. You're creating a monopoly."

Whatever you believe, plug it in here. You'd say to people, "That's not our approach." The way we really believe you challenge the status quo is to let people know that it's a broker-driven model. We've transitioned our model to, *what is it that a risk manager is doing to get a better ROI to lower cost?* As you can see in Graphic 3.4, the risk manager understands an underwriter is going to look at how much risk they see, and they're going to attach a resulting premium or a corresponding premium to that.

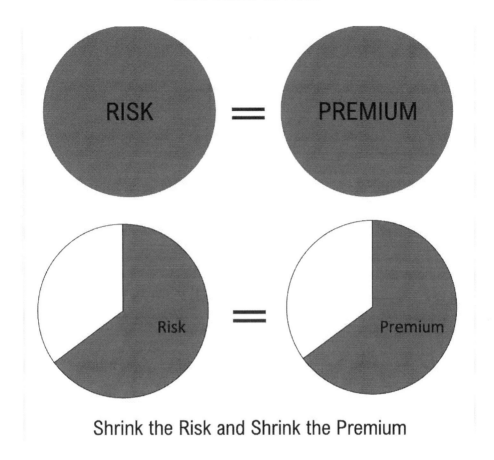

Shrink the Risk and Shrink the Premium

Graphic 3.4

In Graphic 3.4, you can see if you want to cut the premium, you must cut the risk. So a broker takes you to market to get a better deal—the last 60 to 90 days of the year. A risk manager works all year to shrink risk so they can shrink premiums. An underwriter develops a premium by deciding what losses they will see on this account over the next 12 months. They're going to take those losses. They're going to figure it out. If they're going to spend $80,000 on losses next year, then they will add in what they need for expenses and what they need for profit. And that's what they're going to charge in our industry.

Buyers are still so focused on this market mayhem, the belief they can save money on insurance through doing more marketing. That's like saying somebody with a low credit score of 580 and is also unemployed can get a better interest rate by simply hiring more mortgage brokers. Clearly that will not work. Instead, they need to shrink the risk to the mortgage broker or to the mortgage company.

In the mortgage world, how do they shrink the risk? By getting credit scores up and by getting incomes up. So how do we shrink risk? Because we're going to ask people to spend some time with us in discovery so that we can better assess their situation. Spend some time with us, and let us compare your program to the best programs in your industry that have full-time risk managers. They have a huge advantage over you. We're not going to suggest you hire a full-time risk manager. We're going to look for the three or four things that you might be doing, low-hanging fruit that we could take from the risk management model, and what you could be doing if you just knew about them. The problem is we can't guess which ones are going to work the best for you. We don't know you, but we've developed a process, and we're going to show you that in Graphic 3.5. The next step is discovery. And if you look at discovery, that's where we spend about an hour with you, with all your leadership team, everybody that has a stake in this risk.

I want to speak about risk for just a minute more. When you start a business or a nonprofit, you have risk. You have risk with your employees. You have risk with your customers. You have risk with a whole body of people.

If you're out driving in a truck, you have risk with the general public. And so there's a cost to risk. For every dollar at the top of a profit and loss statement, someone worked hard to create that dollar. And risk is where those dollars get siphoned off out of your P&L. If we can shrink the risk, then we can shrink the cost of that risk. If you have a driver on a truck that breaks his or her ankle unloading that truck, your workers' compensation cost may go up. But more importantly, you now don't have a driver on that truck. And there may be a bigger cost to that risk getting those things delivered because we don't have a deep bench of other employees that can hop on that truck. Our model is a game changer. And you producers that are reading this right now, you've got a decision to make. You're going down one path or the other in this business, and you need to make the decision and stake everything on it. Push all your chips on the table one way or the other. You're a bidder. You're going to bid insurance, or you're going to go down this path of understanding, *What investments has my firm already made to shrink risk?*

What investments will we be making in the future? As we learn how to shrink risk, we can literally stake out the only clients we want when we're in the initial meeting—we're not interested in the bidders. How freeing would that feel? We're interested in those that want to shrink risk: less risk, less money going toward paying for risk, whether that's through the injured employee not being injured or through lower insurance costs. In Graphic 3.5, we're showing them the toolboxes we have to shrink risk. And the three most important toolboxes that shrink risk are loss modeling, risk mitigation, and noninsurance transfer. Your firms have already made investments into those toolboxes, and prospects don't like vague promises of how you're going to help them. They want to know specifics so that we can define the toolbox. We can talk about investments our firm has made into those toolboxes because we understand this is what risk managers do all day, all year. They shrink risk. You might say, "So, would you be interested in spending an hour with us in this process we've described in Graphic 3.6 from discovery? You can see we will come back and deliver you a blueprint."

Sample P&C Blueprint Toolbox Graphic 3.5

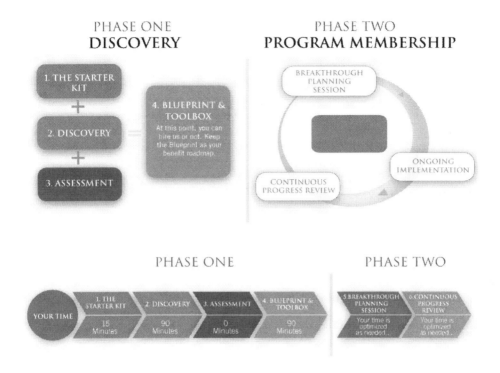

Sample P&C Blueprint Process Graphic 3.6

We continue, "What is a blueprint? It's a form of proposal that identifies the low-hanging fruit to shrink risk and a plan to make it happen. You don't have to hire us to get a blueprint. We don't charge for it. Maybe we should. Right now, we don't. I think one of these days, we probably will. But as of today, Mr. Prospect, we don't charge for a blueprint. So let me tell you, if you want to go through the discovery process, what you're going to get from us, most importantly, we're going to start with just comparing your program with the very best. What that's probably going to yield? Is it going to show areas where you're vulnerable because you don't have a full-time risk manager? That's not your fault. We're trying to close that gap between you and the best. What's the low-hanging fruit that if you had a full-time risk manager, somebody could help you seize upon? And you're going to have a plan that your team can work together to get a greater return on investment on all this risk that your firm has to take on."

"So those are probably the three or four best things that you'll get Mr. Prospect out of going through discovery with us. But ultimately, that's up to you. Would you like to book that discovery meeting?"

We spend hours and hours teaching our clients how to execute this, and you will understand it more as we progress in this book, but for now, go back to the central themes. The incumbent wins 90% of the time on the quote/bid process. The client or prospect loses 90% of the time because of "market mayhem." And so why wouldn't it make sense for you to say, "You know what? I'll never, ever participate in that game again." We've already said we may end up quoting, but we're not going to start with a quote/bid. We're not going to go from first to third base. Mandatory, mandatory, nonnegotiable. We go from first to second base. Even if your best friend started a company and there's no competition, why wouldn't you take them to second base? Why wouldn't you say, "Hey, let me learn everything you've got."

An underwriter is going to be leery of a new company, but if we spend time in discovery, we can learn all the things they're already doing to mitigate risk. Maybe it's their background, maybe it's their bias, maybe it's the resumes of all the people, and they've actually been doing this same type of work for a long time. We've got to meet with them and understand how to tell their story through the lens of shrinking risk so that underwriters don't overcharge them. If you want anything and everything you can do to help a prospect, you've got to take them to discovery to learn. Also, don't forget ideal prospect. You don't want to work with everybody.

We know that a lot of these prospects just want a quote/bid. Risk advisors don't quote/bid. Insurance account managers do. Risk advisors help people mitigate and manage risk, and you can only do that through taking them to second base.

Once you familiarize yourself by taking people through a discovery phase, you will realize that your tools are more valuable when they are more relevant and your wisdom is appreciated. More people will hire you. The right type of people will hire you. A logical reason is that we're weeding out the people who only wanted a quote/bid or they need a third bid. They're not willing to spend a little extra time with us to get it right because they want you to go do a bunch of work for them that they need us to do for them so they can meet someone else's requirements for them to complete a bidding project. That's the good news. Closing ratios go up, clients see you as different and the quality of work you're doing, you're appreciated for, you enjoy more, and ultimately you get more referrals by taking them down this path.

We're trying to change how people view this and talk about it. And we want to become Blue Ocean, where we're actually talking about different things, we're saying different things, we're interfacing with a prospect in a different way, and we get to look unique because we *are* unique and that's really what we're trying to do within the blueprint process. In the initial meeting, we start off differently right out of the gate.

CHAPTER FOUR

The Holy Grail In Sales (Discovery)

We know it may sound like a stretch when we say the title of this chapter is "The Holy Grail in Sales," but let us share with you, in 20 years of riding in the car side-by-side with producers in this industry, whether it's employee benefits or property and casualty, we win business in the discovery phase of the Blueprint process. And again, when we talk about the Holy Grail in sales, what we're talking about is the ability of a salesperson to get real buyers open and honest with you, the advisor, about their current situation and what they would like to see happen and what problems or hassles they would like to see go away.

If we can capture all that, we can create a real proposal that's meaningful, which is what makes it the holy grail of sales. We can create a better plan. We can take their program apart and put it back together the right way. And that's ultimately what a powerful discovery session is all about.

In this chapter, we want to share with you how to facilitate a very meaningful discovery session so that you can better understand what your prospects are dealing with so that you can take all of this investment that you've made in your toolboxes and your staff and all the years of wisdom that you collected so that you can put it to good use. If you are new and don't feel like you have much wisdom yet, because you don't, that's ok. Remember you are one member of a bigger team, and your job is to bring the resources together and to keep deals moving to the point of close.

The Open — Starting a Discovery Meeting

When we talk about the best ways to facilitate a powerful discovery session, it all begins with the right mindset. And that mindset is that this is all about THEM. The more we can disconnect ourselves from the outcome for ourselves, the better it will go. The more we can disconnect from whether we're going to get hired at the end of this, the better our discovery meeting will be. Any sales process you run will always be better if you can make the focus about them instead of the focus being about you and all your "stuff." Remember, we lead to our tools, not with our tools. Discovery is an opportunity for you to learn very important details about them. It is not an opportunity for them to learn things about you (yet!). We're not going to solve problems in the discovery phase of the process. We mustn't do that for several reasons. One reason is, if they say to you, "No one's ever talked to me about that, how would you solve that problem?" The standard answer should be, "I don't know yet. I will know by the time we're done, but I may find something out in the next few minutes that causes me to change my mind."

We want to save the solutions for 3rd base of the proposal (blueprint). One reason is so that we don't commoditize ourselves, but we also want to be able to stack everything we learn up against their incumbent and other competitors we might be competing with on a deal. We're going to learn many things about how your prospect is being served by their incumbent broker through this process, even though we aren't discussing them directly. And when we bring back the proposal, we want to stack all of that against them. The prospect should be able to see, in black and white, how badly they are being underserved. All the things you learn are your big wins coming out of the discovery meeting. And the more we can get in the right frame of mind about what is in it for them—that this is about them and we're going to challenge their way of thinking—the better. We're going to dig in for them to win no matter what, which will produce a better proposal from us and raise our closing ratios. When we look at the history of our company in the past more than 18 years, even when we were just getting started and didn't have a lot of the tools that we have now, our closing ratios, when someone took a prospect through the discovery phase, were very, very high.

Remember second base (discovery) on the baseball diamond?—it's scoring position, and it is in the Blueprint Process as well.

Our closing ratios have been 70% to 80% from the beginning, and it has to do mostly with, first of all, getting in the right frame of mind. It's about them. It's not about us. Taking yourself out of the middle of your thinking and replacing it with your ideal client/prospect is powerful. Everything we have added to the process over the years hasn't impacted closing ratios significantly, but it has had a big impact on the adoption rate at the producer level. We have a paint-by-numbers now. Back then, it was more of a blank canvas, and most people just don't feel comfortable in that environment.

When we rode with producers every day for years, and when we were facilitating a discovery meeting while still in the car on the way to the appointment, we would always remind everyone that this meeting is about them, not about us. In fact, we would always play a little game before we went into a discovery meeting, and the premise was this: *This prospect cannot make us their broker; however, they have paid us $100,000 to take their program apart and put it back together the right way, but we can't become their broker. There's a political reason why we can't become their broker. In fact, the statue out in front of the prospect's building was the incumbent broker who was in a bunker in Vietnam with the owner of the business and pulled him out to safety and got shot in the butt like Forrest Gump on the way back to safety. That's who the incumbent is. But the incumbent is no good. They know he's no good. They just can't get rid of them. However, they're willing to pay us to take their* *program apart and put it back together the right way. And they paid us $100,000 to do it right. So we're going to go in here, and we are going to make a difference. That's our role today. We're going to uncover everything we can about how they're currently doing things so that we can help them moving forward, and they're going to pay us $100,000 for it.*

That's the scenario. It is effective at helping us get into the right mindset. It's about them, not about us.

We want to make sure also that you understand that just because we're going to put their interests first does not mean that we give them anything and everything that they ask for or that we will capitulate to going through the process they want us to use (bid/quote or RFP). That's bad for them and also bad for us. Just because our intentions are really good for them to win doesn't mean we're going to do anything they ask of us. Remember that. We want to make sure everyone understands that as you read this.

So beyond getting in the right mindset for a powerful discovery meeting, we must also start the meeting off the right way. We need to set the stage for how this meeting is going to flow and what we are going to do with the information we glean in our discussions. To do that, let them know where we are in the overall process. Show them the process map and point to the discovery stage so they will be able to see what has happened and what is coming up later.

Mr. and Mrs. Buyer, we are here, and our goal today is to better understand your situation to ultimately take your program apart so we can put it back together in a way that it will perform better. After today the next step in the process (point to the next step) is to bring you back our findings (proposal or Blueprint). We're not going to be recommending solutions today. That will be our next meeting, and we will schedule that before we leave here. Mr. and Mrs. Buyer, our ultimate goal is to help you understand what you could be doing differently, perform better, and compare what that looks like. Also, we want to help you identify financial levers you could be pulling to get a better financial deal and have confidence that you're getting the best one possible. Also, we're going to help you understand how you can take every dollar you are spending and get a much better return on that — multiply the effectiveness of each dollar, if you will.

Lastly, before we come back for our next meeting, we're going to get everyone aligned around a plan to implement. We call it a Blueprint (Roadmap, Navigation Plan, Playbook, etc.).

That is what we're trying to do today, to gather the right information to build you a better plan. I also want you to know, Mr. And Mrs. Buyer, that we are going to ask you things that a traditional "broker" would not ask you. So be prepared for questions that are outside of the normal spectrum. We know you may be thinking, why is he asking me that? Because it's not a typical question, but we're trying to broaden the scope a little here, broaden the viewfinder so that we can understand more about your situation that could impact the plan we put together.

And just so you know, let us explain why we will ask the prospect different things that they're not used to being asked.

Many times, when we would ride with producers, we would ask questions that weren't as direct as the questions they were used to from a broker. We could tell people were wondering, why are they asking me that? What does that have to do with my insurance? And so it would occupy their mind, and we didn't want that to happen. So as a standard part of opening up a discovery session that we will facilitate, we will let them know different types of questions will be coming. It will make sense when we bring back your proposal. By letting them know in advance that we will be asking different types of questions, it will allow them to focus on answering the question instead of wondering why we are asking it.

Let's transition out of the set-up phase of a discovery meeting and into facilitating an in-depth discussion about their situation and getting them talking.

(Employee Benefits written by Chad)

The Middle of the Discovery Meeting

We start diving into their world by opening up with some vision casting. I'll tell you, it is a common piece missing in most sales processes. Salespeople are so focused on finding pain or highlighting a tool they believe in that they miss this step. It is our favorite thing to discuss, and it is exciting for your prospects to look into the future. Also, remember, as we looked at earlier when discussing the Change Formula, vision is a key piece to getting people to overcome their resistance to change.

To get them to start vision casting with us, it can sound something like this:

> *I would like each of you to answer this question. If we were looking down the road two years from now, and you were really excited about some of the outcomes that your benefits and workforce initiatives were getting, if all things were possible, what would some of those things be? What would be happening then that's not happening now? (that could easily be replaced with Insurance and risk management initiatives).*

One time we were facilitating a discovery meeting. This was about a $150,000 revenue account, and there were five people on their side of the table, and the person with the least seniority told us that she didn't know what she could add to the conversation. We said, "Anything that you have to add to where you would like to see this thing going if all things were possible is valuable to us."

And she said, "Well, I spend 80% of my time answering benefits questions from the employees, so if there's a way to get some of that back, that could be good."

And we said, "Okay, great. That is a great thing to understand." And then we looked at the other executives, including the highest-ranking person, the CFO, and asked if we could get that time back that she's committed to answering benefits questions. "Is there anybody in the room that would have better things for her to do with that time?" And everyone started speaking up about different things she could help them with. It made a huge difference in us getting the deal, and the lower-level employee really loved that people were fighting over her.

It's important that everyone in the room answers the vision question. Remember, this is your process. You're the ones making a real investment into them, and it will only work for them and for you if they participate at a high level. Even to the point where if we find people are going through the motions, we can close our notebook and say, "We can't help you if you all won't talk to us. If you would like to stop or postpone the process, we can." That type of thinking might seem risky to you, but it's appropriate considering all that is at stake. Again, if they aren't going to talk to you, they aren't going to hire you.

When they do start talking and telling you something about their vision casting, make sure that you get excited with them. Show some emotional intelligence. They may tell you something that they've been thinking about for a long time that they really want to get done. They just haven't figured out how to do it yet. Get excited with them, regardless of what they tell you. They may tell you they want to implement some better communication tools. Who knows?

When they see you as more of an advisor to employers instead of just a quote/bid, unquote/unbid broker, they will tell you things they wouldn't tell a traditional broker. They're going to say things to you that you might not have an item in your toolbox to fix. That's okay. Get excited with them anyway. That happens quite a bit. It's a good sign when someone tells you what they would really like to see happen, and it's not quote/bid, unquote/unbid, broker related.

As an example, this is something that we hear quite a bit, surprisingly, "We would like to offer more training to our front-line managers. We realize that is a real weakness that's holding us back."

Things like that can happen. Don't shy away from it, even though you don't have employee training as a resource. At the very least, when we bring back their proposal, we can tell them that we'll put together an RFP to help them find some front-line manager training. I even have a client that started a management training division because it was such a problem in their market.

Another interesting fact about discovery is that you hear recurring themes that can inform you of where you need to be making investments in your tools and resources to help your clients so that you can capture the flag in ways that you might not have thought of before.

In vision casting, you want to document everything. If we can put their vision list on their whiteboard or carry a big flip chart in with us and write these vision components down and hang them on the wall with blue painter's tape, then let's do it. Anything we can do to make what they tell us visible and get excited, they will attach us to their vision.

Now let's transition from vision casting to a different component of The Change Formula, the dissatisfaction part. A great way to get people talking about what they're frustrated about is to tell them, "We know when we're talking about employees and rising costs of all of this that there can be frustrations. Nothing is perfect. So let's talk about that. What are the things you find most frustrating about administering your employee health care, employee benefits, and workforce initiatives? What would you say is the most frustrating thing?"

Again, nothing is perfect, but it's a great way to attack that. It's going to be what they're most dissatisfied with. They'll tell you those things, and often in a discovery session, people might be more ready to open up about things they're frustrated with, about their incumbent broker, that they weren't willing to do in the initial meeting or earlier in the process. In fact, it happens all the time.

Don't be shocked when they open up. When they realize cool things that can be happening that aren't, they can start to get more frustrated with their incumbent than they've led you to believe. It happens all the time. Another way to unpack whether somebody's dissatisfied, instead of hitting it head-on and asking them what they're frustrated with, we can ask them, "What are some of the roadblocks that could keep your vision from happening?"

It's just another way to question the prospects about where they might be frustrated or dissatisfied. We're just using a different language to do it. I'm a very optimistic person, so I don't know if I have the language to express that I'm experiencing problems. Problems are not really in my psyche. Frustrations are in my psyche. Roadblocks that are impeding my progress are in my psyche. I don't identify with the word "problems."

Your buyers might be the same way. What's most important is don't worry so much about my exact words but that we have to get people to articulate where they're dissatisfied. We have to get them to articulate their vision for the future. Those are two primary components of The Change Formula that are necessary for people to overcome their resistance to change.

Once we've done a powerful vision casting and identified the roadblocks that could keep them from achieving their vision, we're going to start into the questioning phase that's more specific by toolbox. Whether it's cost containment strategies, benefits administration, HR advocacy strategies, compliance, etc., things that are important but that many people don't do very well in discovery. Our ultimate goal is to figure out how they're currently doing things so that we can bring back a better way for them to do each of those things.

One thing we have created to help you efficiently and in a very structured way understand somebody's situation is the scorecard. You can see in Graphic 4.1(below) a sample scorecard. We create many different types of scorecards with our clients depending on vertical, discipline, or other variables. This is a generic version showing that we're making a drastic comparison. You can see on the left side that their situation is very reactive.

Our benefit programs are fragmented, cumbersome and without focus	1	2	3	4	5	6	7	8	9	10	Our benefit programs are integrated, streamlined and focused
Circumstances beyond our control are forcing us to shift a growing amount of benefit program costs to employees.	1	2	3	4	5	6	7	8	9	10	We are in control of benefit program costs and maintain an equitable financing arrangement with our employees.
Our annual renewal process is reactive and causes anxiety, confusion and frustration	1	2	3	4	5	6	7	8	9	10	Our annual renewal process is proactive, orderly, simple and satisfying
Our employees do not understand and fully appreciate the value of the benefits we provide	1	2	3	4	5	6	7	8	9	10	Our employees understand and fully appreciate the value of the benefits we provide
The presentation, communication and education around our benefits does not motivate and engage our employees	1	2	3	4	5	6	7	8	9	10	The presentation, communication and education around our benefits motivates and engages our employees

Graphic 4.1 Sample Scorecard

On the right side, the ten side, they're proactive about the things they're doing. That is a simple example. They can be long or short, and these are samples of the type of information we can gather. We want them to weigh in on a scale of one to ten. My situation is very reactive. In fact, on the employee healthcare side, their whole process starts when they get a much higher renewal than they expected, and then all these wheels go into motion to get that problem solved. It's very reactive. It's another simple way to get a buyer to weigh in.

Another question that you could put on the scorecard is on the left side, which is the low-performing side, that my program is not very transparent. On the high-performing side, my program is very transparent. It speaks to the idea that they know or don't know why they are paying what they are paying. Those are two simple but different examples of scorecard questions, and we want these people to give their answers independently of each other.

In a perfect world, we would send out the scorecard in advance of the discovery meeting for everyone to fill out independently and return to us. And you can see in Graphic 4.2 (below) how we've taken three different executives' answers to these questions, and we've charted them on this graph so that we can see how everyone has answered to help them create the alignment that is often missing on these things. There's always a lack of alignment, and it does hold these people back, and we're going to help them get that alignment. That's what a scorecard can do.

Our benefit programs are fragmented, cumbersome and without focus	1	2	3 X	4	5 X	6	7 X	8	9	10	Our benefit programs are integrated, streamlined and focused
Circumstances beyond our control are forcing us to shift a growing amount of benefit program costs to employees.	1	2 X	3	4	5	6	7	8 X	9 X	10	We are in control of benefit program costs and maintain an equitable financing arrangement with our employees.
Our annual renewal process is reactive and causes anxiety, confusion and frustration	1	2	3 X	4	5 X X	6	7	8	9	10	Our annual renewal process is proactive, orderly, simple and satisfying
X= Cindy X=Bob X= Susan											

Graphic 4.2

And again, the premise behind the scorecard is, please tell me why you gave me that score. We talk about that and about what they think needs to happen for their score to go up. It's a powerful part of the process to get information quickly.

I recently went through a throat cancer treatment protocol, and every week when I met with my oncologist, I had to fill out a scorecard on a scale of one to ten, expressing how much suffering I was dealing with based on many different variables. It was a fast way to find outliers and put a treatment in place. There are so many things each day that pop up in cancer treatment of this type, and faster, more accurate information is very helpful for the patient.

Whether it was a lack of saliva, mouth pain, anxiety, sleeplessness, or breathing—all these different possible side effects of chemo and radiation each week. That was how they quickly gained an understanding of how my treatment was going. We're using that same efficiency system to find out how somebody feels about a certain area of their business.

Other examples could be someone you know going to a new restaurant, movie, etc. I often ask, "On a scale of one to ten, what did you think about it?" I can understand quickly how they felt about that restaurant or movie or whatever it may be. That's what our scorecard is intended to do—provide some structure and efficiency to a powerful discovery session.

So now we have set the stage for the discovery meeting. We have gone through the vision casting and identified where they're dissatisfied, what their roadblocks are, and what they're frustrated with. We have discussed the scorecard on different aspects of their benefits program and workforce that we need to understand that they need to be aligned around.

I can also go beyond the scorecard and ask them questions to get more depth. Here are a few examples of those, and then we'll give a few examples: "Walk me through how you…" "Tell me in as much detail about how you handle…"

These aren't questions at all; they are statements that are more effective than open-ended questions. They force the person to open up to you in a unique way, and—more importantly—they can't tell you about a process they don't have, which eventually exposes the incumbent.

I also like to ask if there are elements of their program that they like and would like to keep. I would never give a proposal without knowing the answer to that question.

Let me explain what I want you to understand about a discovery meeting. Some of you intuitively know what I'm trying to do here. I'm trying to take their program apart and put it back together. If you write a lot of business by looking at, and reading stop-loss contracts, then by all means, get the stop-loss contracts. Leaving the discovery meeting, nothing is off-limits. Whatever you need to know, the discovery meeting is the time to ask. Because their guard is down. This is the time to ask. Remember, discovery is where we take their program apart, and when we leave the discovery meeting, building their plan is the way we start to put it back together the right way.

The final part of the discovery meeting and setting the next meeting — The Blueprint.

As we wrap up the discovery meeting and we have learned everything we needed to know, we've asked for any documents we need. It could be their enrollment guide, stop-loss contract, HR handbook, etc. There are many things that can give us insight into how they're currently doing things so that we can show how we would improve upon them. What we want to do before we leave is schedule the Blueprint meeting or the proposal meeting before we get out of there. Let them know that the hard work on their part is now finished. Now the hard work for us is beginning. We will spend hours reviewing this information and putting your plan together. It's going to take us some time to do that.

The ideal timeframe to schedule your meeting for the proposal is two weeks. It will be hard to get everybody scheduled exactly two weeks from that day, but I want to give you that time frame as a benchmark because if we bring it back too quickly, we lose some of this power. We lose the mental imagery of us burning the midnight oil, sitting in the conference room with empty pizza boxes, and lying on the floor as we are all exhausted.

At first, when you create a proposal in the way we recommend, it will take some time, but it won't take as long after a few rotations. It'll be much easier by your third or fourth time. There are a lot of items in previous proposals that will stay in future proposals. Even though this is customized, there are very few pieces that we will end up having to customize later—because even the problems that employers are experiencing are the same, not just our solutions. Understand that it will get much quicker to build these. But even when we can do them quickly, we can still create the impression that more work went into it than we actually did.

Just as returning too quickly with a blueprint causes a potentially negative effect, waiting longer than two weeks can also cause a negative effect. When we do that a lot of the emotional information they gave us will begin to dissipate. Two weeks is the perfect time frame to try and reschedule around. You want everybody in the discovery meeting to be in the blueprint meeting. And you need to set up that you're not going to deliver the blueprint if somebody backs out last minute. It's very important that you say whoever is in the meeting now needs to be in the next meeting so that we can maintain our congruency and we're all on the same page. The team we start with is the team we need to finish with. I would ask, "Are we all on the same page with that?" And they nod their heads. Then we coordinate calendars for everybody.

What that sets up for you is that if somebody tries to step out of the conversation later, you can reschedule the meeting because the worst is when the only person that can tell you yes decides to step out at the last minute. This provides a defense for us to be able to reschedule the meeting.

(P&C Discovery Meeting written by Jeff)

So you've got a prospect that has already shown you they're different from a lot of others in that they didn't expect you to just take a stack of documents and go to market. They've agreed to carve out an hour with their leadership team to spend with you. *What is your sole objective here?* To serve them. To help them. If you weren't worried about getting hired, just quit worrying about getting hired. Just serve people. We found that it serves you well. Again, they've already shown you they differ from the average prospect. If we're going to serve them, don't forget we may have some people in this meeting that weren't in your initial meeting. So just remind them, "Hey, we're not here to quote/bid your insurance. We are here to see if we can help you reduce risk and improve the ROI of your insurance program. I want you all to think about this for a second." Set the stage that we're in a business where most people are focused on going to market, which is about one component of managing risk, and that is the transfer piece.

If you want to look at the planet's simplest risk management model, there are three steps to it, and transferring risk is the last step. So first, we look to identify risk, then we look to mitigate that risk, and then we transfer risk. This meeting will follow that format. To provide some structure to the meeting and also get a ton of information in a short amount of time, we will use a scorecard to help. It will also create some alignment on their side that is difficult to get as they all score themselves differently.

One of the most powerful parts about using the scorecard with multiple buyers in the room is they didn't know that others felt the way they did about some of their issues. We get to be the beneficiaries of that. You can see some examples of a commercial scorecard in Graphic 4.4 (below). Discovery is about discovering what you want from your prospect to help them. As EOS implementers, we believe in scorecards of all types inside the agency. They work beautifully for prospects too. If you are too insecure to send it out in advance, we get that too; bring them with you to the meeting, pass them out, and start discussing. You don't have to use a scorecard if you don't want to. It's there to prompt the conversations that will help you identify, mitigate and transfer risk in a meaningful way.

Conservative appetite for risk-We would prefer to spend more on insurance premium and self-insure as little as possible.	1	2	3	4	5	6	7	8	9	10	Aggressive appetite to assume versus insure Rrsk-We would prefer to spend far less on insurance premiums and self-insure as much risk as others will allow.
We do not know if our current insurance program is aligned with the Risk Tolerance of our Leadership	1	2	3	4	5	6	7	8	9	10	Our Current Program is Very Closely Aligned with our Leadership's Risk Tolerance.
We don't know how to use Loss Modeling to leverage insurance companies to lower pricing.	1	2	3	4	5	6	7	8	9	10	We use effective Loss Modeling to help us gain leverage on insurance company pricing.

Graphic 4.4 (Scorecard)

If you think about it, we help people in three ways. You help people through dialogue. If you go to the doctor, the doctor asks what's wrong. They help you through dialogue. The doctor can get your records or documents, but the doctor can also look at you. It's no different here. If we build a blueprint proposal, it will be through dialogue, documents, and what we can inspect with our eyes. So the more they let us uncover and the more they talk to us, the better their blueprint is going to be.

Let's set the stage and let them know what we're trying to do. You can tell them we have some big, sophisticated clients with full-time risk managers, but only 2% or 3% of companies have full-time risk managers. What we're here to do is to compare your program to theirs. We've got a series of toolboxes, and we know risk managers have these tools. We're going to walk through some of these toolboxes and see if you are utilizing all the tools at your disposal for the money you are already paying. *Do you know about them? Should you be using them?* Etc.

Our ultimate goal is to reduce costs by reducing risk. We're going to be able to help you drive greater ROI for this, and it's going to be no burden on you.

As you start the discovery meeting—and this is really fun—we're going to ask a question early that will tell you a lot really quickly and then probe from there with other questions that give us valuable intel about their disposition toward risk and insurance. This is before we ever get to the scorecard. Do they see insurance as transactional or strategic? What's the biggest thing that you worry about happening to this company that could really impair your results? These days we might even have people say a pandemic. We wouldn't have heard that three years ago. But the reason we ask that question is that we want to see if they discuss risk or premiums. If they see this as a transaction, then we've got a little work to do to help them understand that premiums go down when risk is reduced.

We're trying to figure out how the prospect views insurance. We do that by asking a vision question. "If we're sitting here three years from now and celebrating your progress with your risk management and insurance program, what would be happening then? I mean, if it's perfect, what would that look like? What would have to change?" Follow that up with what roadblocks could keep that from happening or something similar.

They will tell you the premium would be lower, or they will talk about safety culture and employees following safety guidelines, etc. You're going to know quickly what you're dealing with.

Early on, we just ask those simple questions: *What do you worry about? What would it look like to have the perfect insurance risk management program? What roadblocks could hold you back?* I promise you will know if they see this as a quote/bid or if they're seeing this as a little more strategic.

Once we have that discussion, we can move to the scorecard. A scorecard is there to prompt dialogue and, most importantly, to prompt the right dialogue. And instead of starting out saying like old-school insurance people, "Can we review your policies?" We go at it from a very different angle. We are trying to make a difference.

We ask them about their risk appetite. One of the scorecard questions we ask as a standard protocol is what their risk appetite looks like on a scale of one to ten. As a follow-up question, we ask them how confident they are that their program aligns with their risk appetite.

What if the business owner and the CFO have different answers? The business owner is aggressive, but the CFO is more conservative. It's always a great conversation; a common response is that they haven't had a conversation like this before.

Maybe the business owner is a nine, and the CFO is a three on the scorecard. We had a producer we work with win a large transportation account, $300,000 in revenue, a couple of years ago because all he had was a high deductible option on auto liability for a transportation firm. The CFO was very conservative, and he felt like, *If I could get to the business owner, I could write this account because his appetite for risk fits this.*

He finally got the business owner engaged. And he was right. He had a greater appetite for risk and loved our producer's program, and we wrote it. Our first goal is to get the business owner and CFO together on their risk appetite so they can build the right plan.

Remember risk management. You identify risk, you mitigate risk, and then you transfer. The most important thing you'll ever do is help somebody identify risk and identify how much of that they want to retain and how much they want to transfer.

Think about this. Until I understand your risk appetite, I don't know how to talk to you about some lines of coverage that some people carry and others don't. Like cyber liability, employment practices, or D&O for a privately held firm.

Once you know their risk appetite, you will talk to them through the lens of that risk appetite. Say, I'm trying to get you to consider some optional coverage that not everybody buys. Once we get that, look for your blueprint. We tell people, "We're going to need a copy of your policies. And all we want to do is report any area where your program is out of alignment with your risk appetite." It will probably be one of those meaningful things you get out of discovery.

Now we're going to talk about losses in the blueprint world. In the typical broker process, people sling losses as fast as they can to get to the market that they think will be competitive, to block everybody else, as we discussed in the initial meeting with market mayhem. But we've got to stop and say, what's an underwriter trying to achieve? I've reviewed so many annual reports, so I know that for most of these insurance companies, before we got to this difficult market, they're just not interested if a risk has a greater than s 50% loss ratio.

We need to slow down. We need to get five years of loss information, and we need to look through that first and understand what the loss ratio is. How's the market going to look at this account? We refer to this process as loss modeling. We ask them head-on to walk us through their loss modeling process, what it reveals, and what changes they typically make when they go through the process.

Most of the time, we get very low answers—twos and threes on our scorecard regarding loss modeling. It's a soft spot in their armor. It's a soft spot for the prospect and their incumbent broker. When we do it this way, we are assuming the role of an educator, an advisor. We are also chipping away at their current beliefs. Everybody cares about premiums, but nobody understands that this is the number one area that's going to determine what they pay. An underwriter looks at how much risk they see in terms of what losses they're going to have. Then they add some expenses and some profit, and that's how the premium the prospect pays is calculated.

When everybody's slinging these loss runs quickly to block the markets without stopping, that would be like swinging a 580 credit report out to several mortgage lenders instead of going, "Wait a second, is there anything we can do to increase this credit score?" Because we're never going to get "A" paper. Losses and credit scores are the same things. A credit score is probably the most important determinant of getting a paper on any loan.

If we can get five years of loss information, think of the things we can do. If you do a five-year premium and loss summary, that is their current situation. In the five-year premium loss summary by line of business, you look at General Liability; what did they pay in the last two years? What were their losses? We lay out every year, and then aggregate that over five years for all lines of business.

Does this account need to be marketed? Does it need to be broken up? Market one line of business separately from the others. Most importantly, loss modeling is a verb. It is active.

We look at these losses to determine if we make this loss ratio look better. How can we do that? Well, number one, we can lower a reserve. Number two, we can explain a shock loss and all the risk mitigation, all the controls that have been put in place to make sure that never happens again. Number three, if there are a lot of claims under work comp for lost time, and you're a specialist at "return to work," we can make some assumptions in the loss model about how much we can cut those if we're looking at a lot of commercial auto claims.

Recently we had a producer working on a deal, and most markets would not quote/bid this commercial auto risk. However, one underwriter did her own loss modeling exercise, and she asked, "Is there any way he would be willing to change the driver profile?"

And the prospect, out of desperation, said, "Yes, what do you want me to do?"

And she said, "I want you to hire older, more experienced drivers."

Now, I don't know how he did that during "the great resignation," but I know he did, and here's why. I know he called his broker back six months later, and he said, "I want you to remarket my account midterm."

The broker was confused and said, "Why would you want to do that?"

And he responded, "Because all my losses have gone away."

This underwriter understood from looking at the losses that they could drive the losses down on this account if he changed the actual drivers. She's using just good practical risk mitigation techniques.

Some other examples of simple, common sense loss modeling methods could be: having one insurance company look at three years of losses instead of five, and the three-year loss pick is much better—that's loss modeling. If you get ten years' loss information, it's a hell of a lot better than the five-year pick, and one underwriter looks at it — that's loss modeling: anything and everything you can do. And as an industry, we miss the boat on this.

After you educate about loss modeling, you will ask for the five-year losses. If we can help them figure out their risk appetite and align their policies, that allows you to see if they have wrong coverages. Not only are you helping them fix their program, but you're bloodying up their incumbent, making it difficult for them to have the confidence they had before you came in with this process with their incumbent. Once we get the policies right (risk tolerance) and go into loss modeling, we can now think of these as two of our toolboxes.

We went through our risk tolerance toolbox to get the policies right. Now we're going to move to our loss modeling toolbox. After that, we moved to perhaps the most important toolbox, risk mitigation. Anything and everything that you can think of that would help mitigate risk. Underwriters want you to shrink risk. The less risk they see, the less premium. Shrinking risk could be helping your client navigate a pandemic, keep a driver on a truck, etc.

Effective risk mitigation impacts their productivity and their profitability. Mitigating risk is good for a company without having anything to do with insurance. When you start a company, you have risk, period. And the more somebody can help you shrink that risk, the better off they will be. Think of it this way: they've got all this top-line revenue they work really hard to create, and all the risk in their company is sucking the revenue out the back door.

It's revenue being lost to pay for risk. The more we can help people shrink risk, the more we can lower their costs and drive a greater ROI. This business is separating. As an industry, we have a decision to make. Are we going to be brokers that sell insurance in a Red Ocean or advisors that help people shrink risk in a Blue Ocean?

We also now have another toolbox, the risk mitigation toolbox. What are the kind of tools and capabilities that might be in your risk mitigation toolbox?

Let's look at commercial auto: It would be questions about hiring drivers.

What does that look like? What are your requirements for hiring a driver? Are they using telematics? Do they have fleet maintenance? We know how to mitigate risk in a discovery meeting. Please give me the top five initiatives you currently have to prevent commercial auto losses. You can ask the same of work comp. What are the top five initiatives you have to keep your people safe on the job?

This is so fun when you get the hang of it. We are really helping people by simply asking them questions that lead to solutions they didn't know existed. Do you have five more? Do you have five that are a lot better? You know what else is cool? If they know more than you, you didn't lose. If they're better than you, you now have a better top five or a better top ten than you had before to use with every other prospect and client.

We have built a Discovery Workbook with a database of possible questions by toolbox, depending on the type of risk. We think it's one of the reasons we get new producers up and running so quickly.

Can you see a Blueprint-type proposal coming together in your mind? We hope so.

Since we can mitigate risk both before and after a loss, we can't forget to dive into Post Loss Risk Mitigation. We have already discussed what someone is doing to prevent the loss, so let's take those same two lines of business, auto, and comp, and look at Post Loss Risk Mitigation. Your competitors often overlook this.

Let's start with Work Comp. An employee has just been hurt on the job. Let's get the prospect to walk us through from the second they got hurt until they returned to work to see if they have already been educated on Post Loss Risk Mitigation or if this is an area we can help them improve.

We are listening for two key items in their program at this point:

1. *Do they have a nurse hotline?* As many as four out of ten claims have been eliminated for many companies by allowing a nurse to direct care. Everything from "Call 911" to "Put a Band-Aid on the finger and let them get back to work." So that's the first thing we're listening for, and many companies don't have that yet.

2. Next, we are listening to see if they have *a sound return to work or light duty policy.* We know that in many jurisdictions, we can get up to a 70% discount off the claim amounts if we can restrict the claim to medical only with no lost time.

Same with Commercial Auto: This question simply asks them to walk you through their procedure when they have an accident. If one of your drivers in a pickup gets in a wreck, walk us through your procedure from the second they step out of the cab of that truck all the way to when the claim gets paid.

Much like Work Comp, you know the procedures your best clients follow to lessen any resulting claim payout. Here are a few easy ones:

1. Don't admit fault
2. Take pics
3. Should they call anyone at your office?
4. Claim advocacy on larger claims

And a reminder, we don't offer solutions during discovery. It'd be just like giving away the end of the movie in the middle. You don't want to do that. You'll screw up your blueprint meeting. They might even ask you, what do you think about our auto procedures after a loss? Please tell them that you don't know yet. Tell them that you are still getting a kind of 360-degree view. Even let them know that you have some people at the office that are specialists at this stuff, so I'm not really prepared to comment on that yet. Let them know that it will be in their blueprint.

Think how different that is from the typical salesperson. When somebody is trying to get them to comment, they want to show how much they know and how brilliant they are. You will never do that again. Make them excited to see the end of the movie… your blueprint.

Now, back to the idea of pre- or post-loss risk mitigation. Anything you can think of that could prevent a loss or hold down the amount of the loss should be discussed now. This is where you'd ask to review employee handbooks if you like to do that. One of the things I like about an advisory sales process like Blueprint is that when you're asking for documents, there's much better context. You ask for policies because you want to see if their program aligns with their unique risk appetite. You asked for losses because you want to do loss modeling to see if you can present a better picture or story to the underwriter.

You ask for their policy relating to sexual harassment, termination, or anything that might create exposure for these people. Maybe it's minutes from a safety meeting or a safety handbook; it can be anything. You might even ask them if there is anything they want you to review relating to safety or any concern. There may be a sell agreement between two partners. Is it structured and funded adequately?

We are not looking to tell you everything you should want to know from reading this book. You should want to know what you want to know based on your firm's tools.

We do want to get you thinking about the toolboxes: risk tolerance, loss modeling, and risk mitigation. When you're out on a job site and observe a lockout tag in a manufacturing facility, you recognize that it would go in the risk mitigation toolbox. The more you can start to place all your tools in the toolboxes, the easier it is to execute the model.

Someone tells you about a really good "return to work" program, and you comment on how effective that is in the Risk Mitigation Toolbox (post-loss). You can then let the prospect know that you have invested in many more tools. Prospects love to know that you've done this before, that it has a structure to it, that you've thought it through, and that the toolboxes and where each of your tools fit make this so much easier for a prospect to gain both trust and understanding in your process.

The last toolbox I'll talk about is the non-insurance transfer. That's just the signing of these hold harmless/indemnity agreements, the requisite insurance requirements, and the certificate tracking that closes the loop.

Underwriters have to know that you've got this handled correctly, or it will result in much larger premiums or in some underwriters simply denying to offer any terms or pricing.

A good example is an agency client of mine that had a prospect who was going to supply lifeguards to one of the top hotels in Las Vegas—a hotel that anyone reading this book would know. They kept getting declinations from underwriters, even those that write insurance for water parks, and it just did not make sense. They finally learned what the issue was, and it was the same for everyone.

The contract between the hotel and the companies furnishing the lifeguards was too vague. The underwriters didn't know what their real exposure was—underwriters like certainty. It's easiest just to pass on the risk altogether, even if it's an exposure you insure daily.

Another example was a general contractor in Missouri who traveled to Texas to complete a project. This created a need for them to buy work comp in Texas. They purchased a policy from the largest writer of WC in the state. At the end of the policy term, they were hit with a $150,000 premium audit. Everyone involved was livid and wanted an explanation, and the carrier let them know that the contract they had in place with their subcontractors did not adequately transfer the comp exposure. The insurance company felt that they had significant exposure for injuries to the sub's employees and wanted to be compensated for that.

In another instance, both a general and a sub were required to carry $25 million limits. Both had the required limits, and the general had evidence of insurance via a Certificate of Insurance. The problem was that they did not have a contract in place.

Why is that so important? Consider the story of the Hard Rock Cafe in New Orleans that collapsed during construction. It's a very sad story due to the loss of life, but also instructive regarding the importance of having contracts in place.

Following the collapse of the structure, pre-completion, three workers were buried under the rubble, one for more than ten months. Can you imagine the finger-pointing and mess following this loss? Who was at fault? Everybody will get named in that litigation, and if your limits are being eroded due to someone else's negligence, what a mess. Let's say the developer or general contractor was not at fault in any way, but how does anyone determine that absent a good contract in place? Obviously, we are not attorneys at Blueprint, but I think it's easy to see what an unmitigated disaster this could be. Bottom line: if not handled correctly, these contracts can create audit premiums or, much worse, impair the limits needed when the really big claim happens.

Using the scorecard approach, we can ask a prospect to score their renewal experience. On one end, they hate the process, and on the other, they love it. This is really telling you what they think of their agent.

It's funny how these scores have a tendency to come back a 1 or a 10. The score is unimportant, but the reason behind it is what we want to discuss. This helps you to really understand if there is an opportunity or if you should walk away. A word of caution, don't forget they scored this before your discovery meeting. You have just had some really good dialogue about all these toolboxes you use to get folks to a better place. It may be fun to ask them to rescore that if they had scored a 10 previously.

And so now, step back and think about the overall approach. Risk managers work to shrink risk all year, not just during the last 60 to 90 days. An advisor is much more than a broker who works the last 60-90 days to collect a check.

Discovery is about really seeking to understand if we can help each prospect. We are putting our servant hat on and digging to see what is really going on, especially as it relates to:

1. Risk Tolerance and whether the program is structured properly
2. Loss Modeling
3. Risk Mitigation both Pre- and Post-Loss
4. Contractual Risk Transfer

The more we get comfortable with our tools and perhaps those we need to acquire, the easier discovery becomes. A real advisor knows where to look to help someone. Keep using the toolboxes; they have a highly structured approach to getting your prospects and clients a much better return on investment with every dollar they spend on insurance.

CHAPTER FIVE

Building A Proposal That Creates Value—The Blueprint

In this chapter, we will discuss how to create a proposal for a prospect that will get you hired. The name of our company is Blueprint Consulting Group. In our world, we call a proposal a "blueprint" for obvious reasons. You can call it whatever you want, but the purpose of this chapter is to try to explain the important components of a good proposal.

First and foremost, a good proposal should always create value. When we talk about creating value, who are we talking about creating value for? We are talking about creating value for our prospect. We're always thinking about them first. *How can we impact what they're doing? How can we create value for them?* Remember, in the discovery phase of the process, we took their program apart, and we wanted to see all the different components of how they were operating and how they are currently doing things. Our goal in doing that is to see if we can improve upon them. When it comes to creating value within a proposal, we have to have a meaningful backdrop for the solutions we recommend. It is what makes our process different from a capability's presentation.

Creating a value-based proposal was why we went through the discovery phase, cast vision, and identified roadblocks by digging into their processes to find flaws. If we didn't go through all the trouble of understanding their situation to find out what they really wanted to see happen, we would have to guess what mattered, and we all know, from first-hand experience, how ineffective guessing is. In fact, if you have the "guessing what matters" skill, you should have thrown this book in the trash a long time ago.

Again, in discovery, we're taking their program apart. A good proposal should put their program back together based on your wisdom and expertise. And the better the discovery meeting you do, the better proposal you can have.

We win business in the discovery meetings. Our proposals should simply confirm the beliefs they have about us already because we're the ones that took the time to care enough to take a deep dive into their situation and help improve it with no strings attached. So how do we create value? Again, it begins with having by being relevant to their situation.

Based on what we understand, we're trying to make their program authentically more effective for them. It's why RFPs don't work as well as the process that we've outlined in this book. The RFP is all about the broker, and it's not anything about the prospect. An RFP is what someone "could" do, but the blueprint process is what we "would" do, and there is a huge difference between the two. This process takes the broker out of the middle and puts the client in the middle.

We get to clarify a prospect's most important goals. We get to understand the roadblocks that can keep that from happening, and then we can build a plan to help them go forth and conquer, and an RFP just cannot do that.

Sometimes your prospect might have to do an RFP as a regular part of their process. Municipalities, schools, and nonprofits are notorious for that type of thing. When this happens, we like to present our process as a companion process to the RFP process, and it tells the other half of the story.

The RFP is about the broker, and our process is about the prospect and everything they need to do differently to get better outcomes. Most of our clients are so ineffective at RFP's they use our process as a litmus test for how serious a prospect is about getting it right. If they are serious, they will do a side-by-side, and we feel like we can stack the deck in our favor, but if they won't take us up on our process, they are likely hiding the fact they need a third or fourth participant in the RFP process, and we politely walk away from those. If you are good at them, then by all means, keep doing them, but our clients moved on from them because they are ineffective at helping the prospect get better outcomes and frankly are the "red ocean."

Let's discuss some simple ways to create relevance in your proposal. Number one, and if you go back to chapter two, where we talk about The Change Formula: an important variable to getting people to change is a powerful vision for the future. It's why this really important question: *If we were looking at two years from now or three years from now. And you were excited about the outcomes that your program was getting. What would be happening then that's not happening now?*

We want to document that vision because we're going to make our tools and resources much more relevant if we do a thorough job of that. We can list that in a proposal as an "opportunity" or desired "outcome" or pick your synonym. Use whatever words you want.

A second simple way to create a powerful backdrop relevant to your prospect is to document the areas where they're most dissatisfied (another variable in The Change Formula).

We document their vision, and we also document where they are frustrated. That could be listed in a proposal as a threat, challenge, hazard, red flag, etc.

Thirdly, a backdrop that can make a difference is documenting what they are good at or what element of their program they want to keep. Similar to other categories, such as an "opportunity" or a "threat," we can list it as a "strength" or something similar.

With any proposal that we give, we should be able to document a few "strengths." It will prove that your proposal is not some type of hot-button presentation but a strategic plan that is meaningful in many ways. Think of it as a framework similar to the traditional S.W.O.T. (Strengths, Weaknesses, Opportunities, Threats) analysis that many business advisors/consultants use. But it also will allow us to enhance something that's really meaningful to them already.

Again, if I'm going to give a proposal to somebody, I would never deliver it without understanding what elements of their program they want to make sure that they want to keep. It could be an insurance carrier, a piece of technology, or an account manager. Who knows what they might tell us, but we need to know before we build the proposal, not after delivering it.

The proposal is built to "seize the opportunities" and "eliminate these threats" to your program, and these are the strengths that we're going to enhance.

After we list all the opportunities, threats, and strengths, we want to park right there and get their buy-in on that list before we get into solutions. That is going to let you know whether you're going to win this deal. It's valuable salesperson intel that you'll get by stopping right there and making sure they give you feedback. Make everyone reply to the question: "Did we get this right? Is the rest of this document built to make these things come to pass?"

We don't move to the toolboxes until they tell us, "Yes, you nailed it." We do not move on with rolling out their plan and the tools to implement that plan until they give us their buy-in.

We can layer in more questions if we like: *Is there anything you would move up or down in priority on this list? Is there anything you would take off this list or add to it?* And then, you need to be quiet and let them answer when you ask this series of questions. If they don't answer you, you need to ask that question again. That is our first "close." It's actually a hard close—it doesn't feel like a hard close to the buyer, but it is.

Their answer will give you valuable intel as to whether you got it right based on what they told you in the discovery meeting. Once they tell you, "Yes, you got this right," often they will say, "I'm not sure why." It's just a common colloquialism. When you really get it right, they say, "You nailed it." It's fun for us when that happens, and it happens often.

One of the first-ever blueprint proposals we did roughly 17 years ago was with one of our favorite clients and a longtime friend out of Michigan. We went through this part of the proposal, and the company's CEO was focused on every word. The CEO's name was Jean. We got along well; in fact, we called her "Jean the dancing machine." She was really bright, and this was a nonprofit.

This was a roughly $125,000 revenue deal, and after walking through the threats, opportunities, and strengths, we simply asked, "Did we get this right? Would you change anything?" And then there was a long pause, and it was a little awkward, but we didn't say a word. (We had made sure before the meeting and shared with the team we were with that when we ask this first closing question, we have to let them answer.)

After a few minutes, she looked up at us over her glasses. They had started sliding down her nose a bit, and she said, "You nailed it." And we knew at that moment that this deal was ours. Or better yet, we knew we could only screw it up from there. It was one of the original blueprints we had done, and so we were still pioneering it, but we knew if we could document how we could help solve the problems that we identified and the key objectives that they wanted to accomplish, we could get hired. We are fortunate that we consistently win business, with high closing ratios, when they tell us, "You nailed it."

Let's look at an outline of the entire process now that we have set the stage for the Blueprint proposal, and we will explain the purpose of each step after that.

Threat 1-
Threat 2-
Threat 3-
Threat 4-
Threat 5-

Opportunity 1-
Opportunity 2-
Opportunity 3-
Opportunity 4-
Opportunity 5-

Strength 1-
Strength 2-
Strength 3-

Every "threat" has a corresponding "opportunity." We never leave a threat unattended. Even if it's something we don't do on a regular basis, it could be something like "We need better training for our managers."

If they say it, we document it.

In the blueprint, we might simply provide, as our solution, an opportunity for us to help them create an RFP for some manager training. We don't need every solution in-house to be valuable to them. 99% of the time, we will have a tool or capability in our toolbox because discovery will lead us there, but sometimes when we ask the vision question, we learn about initiatives that are important to them. This is a good sign that they see you as an advisor instead of a salesperson.

You don't need more than five or six threats or opportunities, and the strengths can be just two or three.

The threats and opportunities should go in the same order, and then as you start presenting the solutions by toolbox, they go in the same order as well.

Here is an example everyone can understand:

Threat — your program has limited cost containment measures being leveraged, causing you to overpay for your insurance.

Opportunity — leverage and alternative funding strategy to create more pricing transparency to lower costs by lowering risk factors.

Toolbox 1 — Cost Containment Toolbox

*This could be many things, ranging from self-insured plans to captives and a host of other ways to lower costs, that you all have at your disposal.

After we go through the Threats, Opportunities, and Strengths, we then present our solutions by toolbox, tying them back to the threats, opportunities, and strengths. We then move to a simple action plan that ties it all together, and it should make it really simple to move forward. Sometimes, if we aren't careful, we can give them too much to think about to make a decision quickly. Because of that, we want to create a simple action plan that shows it's easy to step into this new plan we have created for them. Just 8-10 items in order are fine.

The worst thing that can happen is, "Wow, you've really given us a lot to think about," and if we aren't extra careful, it will happen.

After the action plan, we simply ask, "How soon do you think you should begin implementing some of these solutions to move toward these better outcomes?" It's better if they don't sense we are trying to close them or get them to hire us at this moment. We want the truth, and at this phase, we can get a clear understanding of their urgency with this question, especially if they don't perceive this as a "close." Even though we are closing with this question, we are using softer language to flush out their true intentions.

After the simple action plan, we then move to how they can hire us if they choose to do so. We assume they aren't hiring us on the spot, and we want to use that to our advantage.

We prefer to provide a couple of options at this stage of the close. The first option is for them to make us their broker, and everyone has hired us by making us their broker. However, if you can't do that, then we will do it for a fee of X dollars.

There is some serious psychology behind closing by giving them a few options. Not the least of which is this method diffuses the tension of them firing the incumbent broker. In essence, we are giving them the option to keep them by presenting an option that has a fee closely associated with the commissions. This exposes how little their current broker is doing for what they are being paid, especially compared to what you will do with the proposal you just outlined. Remember, differentiation happens by comparison, and the difference between what you're proposing and what they are getting can be stark.

As a final close, we love to ask, "What would keep us from partnering on this?" We love to ask it more because we are curious instead of because we are trying to get hired. It's actually a hard close, using really soft language that keeps us neutral about the outcome of the deal in their mind, but we get the valuable intel we need to see if any roadblocks could keep this from happening.

We collaborate with our clients heavily because agencies don't compete with each other in our program, and we have created some amazing proposals over the years. If you are on a team that works closely or in some type of non-competing collaboration, we recommend working together to build a database of great proposals to pull from and learn from.

CHAPTER SIX

The Prospecting Effectiveness Formula

This may be the most important chapter in this book because it doesn't matter how great your process is if you can't get in front of new opportunities. Jeb Blount, in his book *Fanatical Prospecting*, says that if you are a producer today and make $300,000 a year, it's because you are willing to put your compensation at risk based on your ability to prospect. If someone else was doing the prospecting for you, Jeb says you would probably be making closer to $100,000 per year, and we have found that to be true.

What does he mean by that? He means only a very small percentage of people are willing to prospect for a living or actually have the skillset to do that. We worked with a young guy in Texas once who was not very successful as a producer, and he was really smart and driven, and it always drove us crazy that we couldn't help him. He went to work for a top-ten broker, and he called us about six months after starting. He said, "I want you to know I've done about $150,000 in revenue already. It was important to me that you know that. I wanted to let you know that I'm not a loser." We knew he wasn't a loser; he was one of the few people we laid awake in bed at night, wondering what was not clicking.

Why couldn't we help that guy? Because he really seemed to have everything. We asked him what had changed, and he said, "The truth is, I'm an oil and gas guy, and I can now tee up these opportunities at my new firm.

In addition to that, there's a guy that works with me in a support role that used to be a risk manager for an oil and gas company. And he said he closes them all when I take him out on these calls. I think I can do a million dollars in revenue next year in new business revenue."

Now, here's a producer that wasn't successful, and now he's telling us he thinks he can write $1 million in new revenue in a year, which for a lot of people is a career goal as a total book of business.

The risk manager probably makes a good living, but he could be making so much more if he were willing and able to prospect. Your job wouldn't be worth nearly the money you can make without your willingness to prospect.

Prospecting probably is love/hate for a lot of us, but it should be mostly love. If you make a good living in this business, it's because you're willing and able to prospect. We are no different. In fact, any salesperson is in the same situation. It's why we always talk about how we're all pursuing a Ph.D. in prospecting, and you should be, too. We teach a course called Prospecting Ph.D., which you can find at www.prospectingphd.com.

Why Ph.D.? Well, think about this. In your undergraduate courses, you mostly read a book, and then you regurgitate what you've learned by taking a test. Well, a Ph.D. is very different. You're reading all the material, but you're out in the real world. You're out working with companies to execute business, marketing, or technology plans. And so, a Prospecting Ph.D. would encompass the book knowledge, which we need to read books like *The Obstacle Is The Way, Extreme Ownership, Discipline Equals Freedom, Financial Prospecting, Purple Cow, The Compound Effect, Networking Is A Contact Sport*, etc. as well as doing the prospecting on a regular basis. So our hope from this chapter is that you will forever be in pursuit of your Prospecting Ph.D. It's how and why you will create wealth in this business if you are able to do it.

We have determined a formula for you to create wealth and be highly effective at prospecting. We call it the Prospecting Effectiveness Formula, and it reads like this:

Mindset x Skillset x Cadence = Prospecting Effectiveness.

Take a few minutes and score yourself on a scale of 1-10 in each category and see how you do. If you score a 10 in each category, your score will be 1,000.

Mindset

First, let's discuss some of the attributes on a growing list that a salesperson with a strong prospecting <u>mindset</u> possesses:

- They have a 10-year vision and a 3-year vision for the growth of their books (the fuel of the flame of desire), and those visions help determine their annual goals. A person with a tough prospecting mindset will have goals that are always bigger than what a sales leader or mentor would have for them.
- Every call is an opportunity to learn and feed our growth mindset.
- They don't think prospects owe them anything.
- They don't accept people not calling them back, they get creative, and most people call them back.
- They aren't looking for prospects that are unhappy with their current broker. They are looking for clients that want to perform better.
- They read books that make them better and feed their toughness mindset (at least ten pages a day).
- They likely have a vertical or expertise they have developed.
- They hang in there longer on a sales call than others.
- They know where call reluctance comes from, and they learn to overcome it.

- They check their intent always. They typically want to help people perform better and don't lead with their tools and their "stuff."
- They know who their ideal prospect is and have a list of them.

We've always studied prospecting, but it became exponentially more important in March 2020 when the COVID-19 shutdown happened. Our clients froze. We think it's because they are great people with good values. But questions arose, like is it even ethical to prospect during a pandemic? People were freaked, and some of them were losing loved ones and co-workers, and no one really understood the situation. And then the lockdowns came.

Ultimately, we arrived at the answer: if you're calling with help, then hell yes, it's ok. In fact, we need to be helping people every chance we get. It's how we should prospect, anyway. It's a mindset, for sure. Consistently the people we meet that are the most successful have a mindset to help people.

We have a client whose prospects are in the aviation industry, and they were not eligible for PPP loans. They were covered under the Cares Act. And somebody in the government administration had commented that they weren't eligible for these forgivable loans, and he figured out they were. Well, he unlocked $20 million worth of forgivable loans for some of his prospects and clients. If that's what you're doing, it's okay to call somebody in a pandemic.

Do you remember the devastation of Hurricane Katrina on the streets of New Orleans? We wanted to be like those amazing people in Louisiana and other states that were taking the flat-bottom boats out of the rafters of their garages and floating down into flooded areas, passing out water and life vests, etc. We didn't want to be one of those people standing at the water's edge with generators they were selling at three times the retail cost.

If our intent is good when we are prospecting, if we have good news for people in bad situations, and if we bring value to people, then we should be prospecting, and it will work. The helping people mindset works even in good times and helps eliminate people's call reluctance.

We had a young sales candidate take a call reluctance test, The SPQ Gold. It helps us understand where our call reluctance comes from. The good thing about call reluctance is we're not born with it, we develop it, so if it's learned, it can be unlearned. If you're like us, you would think call reluctance would come from fear of rejection. As we mentioned before, surprisingly, his came from having no vision/goals for his future. If a salesperson is missing that part of the mindset, they just aren't going to fight through the knockdowns this job can have each day. These things power us through prospecting a bunch of people telling you, "I don't want to talk to you." "I hate you." "Quit calling me." "I love my current provider." Therefore, the mindset becomes foundational to success.

All three variables of the prospecting effectiveness formula are important and interrelated, but it all begins with mindset. Your mindset can improve as your skillset improves and your cadence kicks in, but if you do the mindset work on the front end, you can expedite the timeframe on growth.

Skillset

Our most common coaching requests are skillset related. You can't imagine how many times we are asked, "Will you give me a script so I can improve my odds of booking a meeting when I am speaking with a prospect for the first time?" It's important that you are on solid ground in that regard. However, we will make a case in the next chapter that the script problem, as important as it is, isn't the biggest problem salespeople face. Think about how much your mindset will improve your skillset and how much better any skillset gets with more repetitions (cadence).

Skillset, at its core, is the ability to build a list of prospects that you really want to work with, and get into a conversation with them, and then, when you do speak with them, be able to convert them from a conversation into an initial meeting. In his book *Book Yourself Solid,* Michael Port speaks about the importance of standing on solid ground when you get into a conversation with a prospect. You need to know what you're going to say. The ultimate indicator of a highly effective skillset is that you're confident that when you get a prospect engaged in a conversation, you can convert them to a meeting at a very high percentage. <u>To repeat: Highly effective prospectors know how to build a list of ideal prospects they want to sign as clients, they know how to get them on the phone (or in person if canvassing), and they know how to convert those conversations into appointments at a very high percentage.</u>

We will be giving some very effective tips to do all of this later on in the book. We won't be discussing all of them because this book would be 500 pages, but we will look at some unique methods we use every day that will work for you. If you know prospecting is a big issue for you and you value learning about different ways to do it, you would probably really benefit from our year-long prospecting class that you can investigate by visiting www.prospectingphd.com

Let's talk about list building for a moment. When we look at list building, so many people start building lists through the lens of a cold call. When we build a list, we start with the accounts in your agency that can be cross-sold. I want to talk about the cross-sell for a second, which we call "cross-serve." Getting in front of an existing customer is a lot easier than getting in front of somebody that doesn't know you. That's obviously common sense. When we meet a banker or a CPA, we build a relationship with them through what we think of as wine and dine. Well, we need to wine and dine the producers inside our own firm.

If you're a P&C broker, wine and dine the EB broker or the surety broker. If you're the EB broker, wine and dine the P&C. If you lived in Dallas, you would take a CPA or a lawyer to a Mavericks game; we'll take the EB broker to a Mavericks game. We want you to think about this as you build your prospect list. The first component of a good skillset is to think of what the easiest way is to get in front of our prospects. What will be the easiest, quickest way to get in front of them but also to make them a client? We will eventually work our way out to the most difficult method, which is cold calling. The point we are making is depending on how we approach a prospect has an impact on the likelihood of us writing them and how quickly.

Our favorite ways to build lists for cold calling in this industry would be MiEdge, Zoominfo, and Sales Navigator. Those are the three tools you need in your tool belt if you're building a cold call list, but you start with other customers in your firm. Make those your customers. A lot of people in your firm need to be wining and dining the other side of the house. Take that to a new level, make that a skillset of yours, and blow up the cross-serve while everybody else makes a bunch of cold calls.

The second thing is to use LinkedIn Sales Navigator to build a second-degree list to make list building easier and more accurate. We're going to talk about that in a later chapter, what we refer to as a referral out of thin air. Use your clients and people that you know from your personal life to get in front of people you don't know. We're trying to convince you to quit rushing to build lists from cold calls.

Now, the next part of the formula is getting people on the phone and then getting them to meet with you. We're going to talk about that in later chapters, but right now, I want to talk about the third formula, which is cadence.

Cadence

In most books you read, there are a couple of stats, and they're different in different books, but you'll read things like this: 47% of all salespeople only reach out to a prospect once. And yet it takes seven calls to a prospect for them to remember who you are and what you do for a living. That's where cadence comes in.

Here's the most important thing about cadence: If you wanted to sell your home today, what are the odds you would reach out to a realtor you don't currently know? When we ask that question, most people say it's zero or close to zero. We all know realtors and would probably reach out to someone we know. Well, let's ask this question, if you became unhappy with your incumbent broker, what's the probability you would reach out to a broker you don't know? We think the answers are very similar to the selling your home question. Brokers are calling on people they're interacting with every day at their country clubs, leveraging COI's and working in nonprofits etc. Jeb Blount says prospecting is nothing more than building familiarity with a prospect so that when a buying window opens, they think of you.

Here's the other interesting thing about cadence. We've got some data that we believe if you were able to get ten people on the phone today, only two of those would probably meet with you.

Eight of those probably would not. No matter what you say or how great your value proposition is, it has nothing to do with you. It's where they are in life. It's what mood they're in. It's how busy they are. It's a lot of factors you don't control. And so here's what's interesting. Think of one group of people that are sitting in this home. Eight out of ten are sitting in this home that won't meet with you for any reason. Two out of ten are sitting in this home and will meet with you the day you call. Here's what's fascinating. Those people are switching those homes all the time, therefore having a repeated, consistent way to stay in touch with target prospects, people that you know you would like to add to your book of business. Cadence is the way we stay in touch with them. One of these days, we will all be on cadence. One of these days, we will be using technology to automate our voicemail and email cadence to make all this so much easier. But right now, cadence is the ability to stay in touch with your target customer so that when a buying window opens, they think of you.

To make this easier, the compound effect creates all these latent opportunities today, but they will show up a little later. The way anything works is by building a relationship with someone so that at the right time, they're willing to talk with you. And so, really, what is cadence? It's making calls every week. The best cadence formula we've seen looks like this. Making calls on Tuesday and Thursday mornings, whether that's 30 minutes or 3 hours. And then go back to building the list, loving on your list. Every Friday morning, every book we read, whether it's *Atomic Habits* or *Deep Work* or *The Compound Effect*, will tell you this discipline will let you down. What you can depend on are habits. Why not just make the commitment today? The way you're going to build a skillset is through cadence. You are going to create an assembly line for prospecting.

What's an assembly line? An assembly line has these processes and inputs, and that assembly line runs 8 hours a day, 16 hours a day, 24 hours a day. We're asking you, *Do you want to solve every problem you have?* Think about this. What would there be to dislike about any sales job if your pipeline was always overflowing? Well, cadence is the key to establishing the assembly line. We help people establish assembly lines for prospecting. They're running when your pipeline is empty. They're running when your pipeline is full, instead of it running in fits and starts when you're in the mood to prospect, the most effective prospectors make it a lifestyle. They prospect in good times and in bad. They're never worried about their pipeline. They're never worried if their largest customer fires them. That happens primarily due to a change of control. What industry hasn't been impacted by being rolled up by private equity firms or the CFO moves? A new CFO comes, and he's got a relationship with a large broker. If we can get the cadence right, and by the way, how do you build a skillset through cadence? Through making calls? We build a skillset.

What happens as my skillset gets better? My mindset gets better. Well, what happens when my mindset gets better? I use cadence, and I make more calls because I'm feeling more confident. These are all interrelated.

Now that you understand the prospecting effectiveness formula, score yourself. Those of you serious about getting your Ph.D. in prospecting at the end of each month, put it on your calendar for the first Monday of each month to give yourself a score. How you did with prospecting effectiveness, paying particular attention to cadence. Because I'll tell you, if your cadence is there, it's a little bit like this. My wife comes home from work. We've been married for 32 years, and my mood determines how I treat her when she walks through the door. Well, let's flip that. Let's say I'm going to treat her how she should be treated and how a great husband would treat her, and that is going to actually impact or direct my mood. What's my point? Make the calls and let the calls determine your mood. Don't start with, *What mood am I in? And should I make the calls?*

Here's what we know: Salespeople, if they know who they are going to call next week and they know what they're going to say to them next week, they're more likely to work the cadence each week. That's where tools like SalesLoft come in and make this really easy because we can take the guesswork about the work that we need to do next week.

In our cadence, we tend to our list on Friday afternoons for the next week, and then Tuesdays and Thursdays, we make our cadence calls. Again, cadence is about the repetition of staying in front of certain prospects that just aren't going to respond to you no matter what you do until a buying window opens. We've seen cadence transform salespeoples careers in just over 90 days by putting 40 new prospects into their cadence per week. And in 90 to 120 days, they have to back away from putting 40 new prospects in their cadence because their pipelines are overflowing. cadence is often the missing piece.

We read a statistic recently, and We've read these types of statistics many times over the years, that 48% of salespeople try to get a prospect on the phone one time, and it takes multiple times to be able to do that. That's where our cadence comes in. It doesn't have to be this huge, monumental reach out. We just need to stay in touch with people so that they think of us when a buying window opens.

CHAPTER SEVEN

Hidden In Plain Sight

It was around 2008 when we recognized that our clients had a challenge hiring sales talent. They all wanted to hire sales talent. It's hard to hire one of your competitors because they've got an employment agreement, and it makes it difficult for them with their book of business encumbered. Or we can hire them, but they end up not being very good.

The next best thing for us was finding what we would call professional salespeople. These are people who knew that becoming a top-notch salesperson was their path, and they took it very seriously. They believe in training and likely already had a bunch of it. They know how to prospect and lay out a value proposition. They also know how to use other team members to help educate and close new business. In an interview, they knew what numbers to track, and they knew them cold without looking at a reference. Typically, we looked for someone that had five to ten years of sales experience with strong B2B prospecting. Sales is in their DNA. And so we decided we're going to step into this producer talent void and go help our clients recruit sales talent from other industries.

Our experiment was to pair them with a closer/mentor, and if they can tee up some appointments, the mentors can help close them, and they can learn in front of a prospect how to close business. Everybody wins.

The idea was to teach them the business with opportunities they create, but there was an issue. We knew that if this new producer was prospecting and we were going to help them figure out this business, we needed more data than the industry normally supplied. And that led us to think about lead indicators.

You've probably heard of the *Lead* versus *Lag* indicator. A Lag indicator is the last thing that shows up. Lead indicators are those behaviors or things we can do to create the Lag we're looking for.

Think about weight loss. If you want to lose weight, the Lag indicator is what the scale is telling you. But we know we can't lose weight by standing on a scale. We know that we've got to focus on calories in and calories burned, regardless of what weight loss program we choose.

Let's pretend to make this simple. We needed one appointment a week above, say, $10,000 in revenue. Don't get hung up on the numbers. Just follow the logic. If somebody walked into their Monday morning sales tracking meeting, every Monday morning, they're sitting down talking about their previous week's prospecting. We're focusing on the Lead indicators. If you were coaching a young salesperson and they didn't get an appointment one week, and you asked them to get one appointment, the Lag, in this case, the one appointment, what questions would you ask? Normally, I would ask them, "How many calls did you make?" "Hey, what kind of things were you hearing?" "What kind of objections?"

And so, we decided to track these lead indicators to help somebody establish benchmark data about what a new producer should expect. Even during the interview process, somebody may ask us, well, how many appointments are you going to expect in a week? And how many calls is that going to take? We knew we needed this data, and nobody had it. And so we developed this producer activity sheet.

In the beginning, we had people we had recruited in a pool, but we also added about 90 other producers in the program that were within their first year because we knew we needed more data. And we will never forget what good news it was that if you look at this sheet, we have three metrics: attempts, conversations, and appointments. Our young producers only had to get five conversations to create one appointment. That metric has held steady to this day.

You think, *Wow, this prospecting thing should be easy. If I need one appointment, just come in and make five calls.* And anybody who has prospected for more than a day knows it's not that simple. This is one of the big takeaways, and it's the reason we name this chapter "Hidden In Plain Sight." This data for some reason, nobody talks about it. The five-to-one metric isn't broken. There's nothing wrong with that. Let's say you were trying to get five appointments a week, and you made five calls, and four people treated you terribly, but you got your appointment with one; that would be great. A five-to-one metric won't run anybody out of this business. But there's another, bigger problem.

If we move left so that the conversion rate of five conversations gets one appointment—that's a 20% conversion rate. There's nothing wrong with that. However, there is a severely broken metric, and that is the number of attempts it takes to get into one conversation. We rarely get a coaching request in our firm to help somebody improve the metric from attempt to conversation. The coaching requests we get are about overcoming objections.

Let's say we get somebody on the phone who is trying to improve the metric of conversation to attempt. There's nothing wrong with that. And if we could create two appointments from five conversations, our book would be twice as big. But we can't manipulate people. We're only going to get the conversations we can get.

Let's look at why this metric is so bad—20 attempts to get into one conversation. Why is it so bad? We think the primary reason is voicemail. We believe people don't take incoming calls, which is why getting people on the phone is so difficult.

An example: I had a young lady reach out to me last year, and she said, "Jeff, I need some help with my script." Now, she's asking about her script, and that's her language, not mine, but we don't script people. If she's asking about her script, she's worried about when she gets somebody on the phone, a conversation, creating an appointment. She's worried about that metric that's not that broken.

I said, "Great, we'll have that conversation. But do you have your data from last week?"

I love this. She immediately said to me, "I made 188 calls that yielded seven conversations that yielded one appointment."

It's so funny how close that tracks to our metrics of 20-to-one and five-to-one. And so I said, "Hey, I'm willing to have a conversation about your script, which is your seven-to-one conversion, but are you willing to have a conversation about the fact that you reached out to 188 people and you only talked to seven of them?"

She said, "Absolutely."

So we have our conversation. She reaches out a few weeks later and says, "Hey, I want you to know I made 22 attempts, got into seven conversations, and got four appointments." That was so rewarding for us to hear. And we would ask you this question. Have you ever tracked how many calls it takes you to get somebody on the phone? Because it's enlightening. We don't track things just to track them. We recommend tracking so you can predict a better future. This metric is hidden in plain sight, and it turns out it's like gold just lying on the ground. Get this fixed, and the results will change immediately.

One reason prospecting is so difficult is your prospect is hunkered in a bunker. And this bunker has a name. They are protected down in a war-like bunker; they're protected from salespeople. They don't want to talk to salespeople. Gatekeepers have been charged with keeping the gate. Don't let anybody pass here. And so, to understand the name of the bunker, we would ask this question, what's the opposite of love?

And our instant reaction is hate. And it may be, but we think of love and hate as extreme emotions separated by a thin line. Think genius and insanity. They're extreme emotions. What we believe is that the opposite of love is indifference, not hate. This is why we call it The Bunker of Indifference.

If you were at your 20-year high school reunion and somebody said, "Do you remember Tom Johnson?"

And this girl says, "Oh, yeah. I hate Tom Johnson. I never liked Tom."

Maybe that's the opposite of love, but really what we think is the opposite of love is someone saying, "I don't remember Tom." We believe that's a bigger slight. This bunker that your prospects live in, and they don't let any salespeople down there, it's a bunker of indifference. You don't exist to them. That bunker is built to protect you. The problem is we keep trying to go in the front door of that bunker. It's heavily fortified to keep salespeople out. But there's a little secret. That lady that went from 188 to seven conversations metric, she improved that to 22 attempts and seven conversations. She quit trying to go through the front door that's so heavily fortified. The back doors are wide open; the side windows are wide open. And with a little bit of coaching, she was able to focus on that metric. This chapter is really about what we've always been told—if you want to improve something, you measure it. And yet most people don't measure attempts, conversations, and appointments.

And by the way, when I've been talking about making calls, I know that some of you are out working. You're out knocking on doors and seeing people. That is the same as an attempt on the phone to us. When you bring somebody in from another industry, and everybody depends upon them making it, and they've got to demonstrate that they can prospect, you have to have this data. We're suggesting you take a three-by-five index card and tri-fold it. It will create three segments, and on one segment, use tick marks for attempts, the middle segment use a tick mark for conversations, and the right segment for appointments.

If we're going to get our Ph.D. in prospecting, we have to get better at simply getting people on the phone. It is the metric that is hidden in plain sight that makes the biggest difference. And as we get better at getting more people on the phone, then we actually get better at having the conversation, and we will begin to convert those at a higher percentage as well.

Whether you're a new producer or a more seasoned producer that's lost some clarity about how to grow, we can predict a better future if we understand our metrics around attempts to conversations and conversations to appointments. It will become a competitive advantage for us within our firm and within our geographic space or our vertical industry. We will have a competitive advantage if we understand what that lead indicator is.

We are fortunate to have this unique vantage point where we get to see people that understand the power of this and see that they win at a higher rate than those that don't. It will actually reduce stress when we understand how many appointments we need each week, whether it's one appointment, two, or three, depending on the environment you're in, when we know that number, we have a much better chance of winning. It also reduces stress because we're inputting the appropriate amount of effort into our prospecting assembly line each day, each week, each month. And we get to fully leverage the compound effect of doing the right things every day to be able to grow our business in a very meaningful way.

Ultimately, the point of this chapter is to help people understand that there are simple metrics to create an easier, more effective way for you to predict a better future and get in front of a lot more opportunities with a lot less effort.

CHAPTER EIGHT

Cold Calling Using A Creative Drop And How To Create A Referral Out Of Thin Air

Even though this is not a book about prospecting, we think it would be a huge mistake not to at least address the issue.

We think you have to have some of the key components working in your favor. So, in this chapter, we're going to try to give you some of our best prospecting tips and tools, things that perhaps you have not ever heard before, that our clients are using and making work for them on a daily basis. So, first, let me just start with a couple of high points.

If we're talking about prospecting methods that we teach and collaborate on, this could be a 25-chapter, 500-page book. In fact, we teach a yearlong course on prospecting called Prospecting Ph.D., and there is a lot to it.

We do think it's important to understand how to avoid the call reluctance that comes with prospecting.

So, when we think about the three variables that impact prospecting, your mindset, your skillset, and your cadence, think of these as an algebraic equation. If you could have a score of 10 in each of these three variables, the highest score you could have would be 1,000.

If you had a 10 in mindset attendance skillset and a 10 in cadence, you'd be the perfect prospector.

Unfortunately, very few of us have all three of those things mastered. The way we prospect has a lot to do with how successful we're going to be. If all you did every day was try to prospect with a cross-sell or call your existing clients, to try to sell them another line of business, then prospecting would be very easy. Prospecting would be easier if you had a CPA or a lawyer constantly introducing you and the ideal prospects. So how will you prospect?

Another issue would be if you're working in one industry or vertical with strong networking partners, you may even have a leads group.

So, the point is all prospecting is not the same. There are so many different ways to prospect.

Think of a cross-sell as a six-inch putt and a cold call to somebody that doesn't know you as an 18-foot putt. We want to try to do everything we can to make sure we're doing these shorter putts.

If we're effective at it, and we're confident, and the plot's not so difficult, we're probably going to do more of it, and it's easier to get in front of somebody with a center of influence or cross-sell.

Not only is it easier to get in front of them, it's also easier and faster to write the business. You just have more credibility when they meet you.

We mentioned in an earlier chapter the biggest problem with prospecting, whether you've been doing this one month or ten years, is getting someone to engage in a conversation with you, whether that's dialing the phone and not being able to get anybody to answer on the other end, or stopping by people's office and trying to get them to engage in conversations.

Remember, the most important metric that we want you to take out of this book is it takes 20 phone calls to get into one conversation, but it only takes five conversations to get into one appointment.

As we're on the journey to help our clients get a Ph.D. in prospecting, we spend a lot of time trying to help people work on that first metric—attempts to conversations. Instead of reaching out to 20 people to get one person on the phone, what if we could reach out to 20 people and get ten people on the phone? This is literally career-changing or life-changing.

How do you get more people to engage in dialog? We talk about two words that come to mind: curiosity and reciprocity.

Think about this:

Say I was prospecting an executive at a large company that doesn't know me, and I knew they went to the University of Texas in Austin and they don't take calls from salespeople, but I decide that I'm going to send them a life-size ice carving of the University of Texas Longhorn mascot Bevo, which is a 2,000-pound steer. So I send this full-size ice carving to their lobby, in the reception area. I call the gatekeeper, and I ask for Mr. Big. I say, "This is Jeff Jenkins. May I speak to Mr. Big?"

They'll probably ask me, "What's this regarding?"

I will simply say, "Hey, I know Mr. Big went to the University of Texas. I sent over an ice carving of Bevo today, and I was just calling to make sure that he got it." I pause for a moment, and I say to the gatekeeper, "You know what? Can you just give me Mr. Big's voicemail?" I get his voicemail, and I say, "Hello, Mr. Big. I had an ice carving of Bevo sent over to your office today. I know that you're a University of Texas graduate, and I'm calling to make sure you got it and ask you to give me a call back when you have a second so I can explain why I sent that."

If I were to ask you this question, as the reader, would you call me back? If you got a life-size ice carving of your mascot, a tiger, a kangaroo, an elephant, or whatever your mascot, and someone literally sent that to your office and called and left you that voicemail, would you call them back?

We ask 20 people in our workshops, "Would you call me back?" And I think the smallest number we've ever gotten to that question is 13. Remember, the typical metric is if you called 20 people and left them a voicemail, one of those would call you back.

Here, the numbers we see are 20 ice carvings. At a minimum, 13 people out of 20 say they would call us back. You're probably not going to really send an ice carving, but we may be able to think of something like that.

Now, why did Mr. Big call me back when I left the voicemail? The answer to this question, you probably know, is curiosity. Curiosity is the greatest way to get people to call you back. If you call someone and leave a voicemail, they only call you back because they want to or they have to. Everybody's busy. Everybody's overworked. We have a lot to work through. Their family, their spouse, their children, the board, maybe their church, employees, friends, family, etc. We've got to cut through all of that and make somebody want to call us back. The fastest way to do that is with curiosity because we're curious beings.

Now, we've learned that when we use someone's alma mater, like their university, it also drives some level of reciprocity. We went to some trouble. We know something about them. We're about to lay out some of our favorite cold call methodologies, which we call our ice carvings. If you want to get somebody on the phone, you've just got to figure out what you could send them to make them curious. What would create curiosity somewhat like that life-size ice carving of a beaver or a longhorn?

At our company, if we can't get in front of somebody with an introduction or referral, we quickly move to an ice carving. Now, we also call these creative drops. We have some of our favorite creative drops, but it's just so easy to go into Amazon and look up the University of Alabama or Notre Dame and find a bunch of unique gifts that are under $10 that we can send somebody to create some curiosity and reciprocity.

One of our favorite stories is about a producer who was more than 60 years old with a $1.5 million book of business. He wasn't that motivated to prospect, but he thought, *This is easy. I will at least try it.* So, he went on to his favorite prospecting resource MiEdge and found ten companies that would generate $100,000 in revenue if he were to win those accounts. Then he went to LinkedIn Sales Navigator and figured out who the CFO was of these ten companies. He was also able to find out what college they attended. This was in August, which made it the perfect time for him to appeal to the football fan in each of the CFOs. He then sent each a hooded sweatshirt with their alma mater printed on it. Some of these were sent from Amazon. Some were sent from their college bookstore. These colleges were Pac-12 schools such as USC, UCLA, Washington, Oregon, etc. So when the prospect received the hooded sweatshirt, they didn't know who it had come from.

That's the curiosity piece.

The fact that it was their alma mater, which many people love. That's the reciprocity piece.

So when he called the gatekeeper, he just asked for Mr. Big, the CFO. Many of them took his call. He left a voicemail for others and said, "Hey, I'm the guy that sent you the USC hooded sweatshirt. I was just calling to make sure you got it, and that you knew why I sent it." He would then leave his cell phone number.

We were amazed that he talked to all ten of these CFOs. In addition, he booked four on the first call with them, and others were willing to speak later. All of this happened from idea to booked appointments in two weeks.

He probably spent about $1,000. But again, he has a large book of business and is very confident in his abilities. The revenue represented by the ten CFOs' accounts would be $1 million.

So, you can see, the thousand dollars could pay a radical return on investment. Had he put his business card in there with the hooded sweatshirt, then he still would have had the reciprocity piece—somebody did something nice for them. But he would have lost the curiosity piece.

We've learned through trial and error: If you put your business card in with a creative drop which is what we also refer to as the ice carving, it ruins the curiosity piece. And we can estimate at least 50% better results, probably more. We believe the moment they know you're a broker, they're probably not going to call you back.

The gatekeeper often asks you what this is regarding, and it's really easy and simple. When they say, "What's this regarding?" We would say to the gatekeeper. "Please just reference the USC sweatshirt. He'll know," or "Please just reference the Oregon sweatshirt."

It's a very easy way to get a gatekeeper to put you through. These are magic words when you're talking to gatekeepers.

"He'll know" or "She'll know."

One of the reasons we had to develop this methodology is that our clients were being greatly hindered by voicemail and gatekeepers.

Twenty or thirty years ago, you could learn to build a relationship with Mr. or Mrs. Big's executive assistant, and they would actually help you and advocate for you to get 15 or 20 minutes.

With Mr. or Mrs. Big, we don't have that anymore, so it's difficult to come up with anything that works with voicemail.

You should challenge us on this. Find 10 or 15, or 20 creative drops. Send them to your target CFO or business owner, no card, no nothing, just curiosity and reciprocity.

The more you can find something that ties to them, the more you're going to have reciprocity working for you.

The creative drop solves a couple of problems. This is really a cold-call strategy. One of the reasons we like it is that call reluctance can be formed by making a lot of calls and nobody calling you back. This will help us solve that problem. Another reason we have call reluctance is we get a prospect on the phone. And we can hear the disappointment in their voice when they realize they got stuck on the phone with a salesperson. The creative drop can really help with this.

Early in the call, if we can just talk about the creative drop a little bit to build rapport before we reveal that we're a salesperson, the better reaction we may get from the prospect. It's a built-in pattern interrupt which we will discuss in the next chapter.

The longer you can build a little bit of rapport around the creative drop, the better it's going to be. When you do reveal that you're a salesperson, if they've relaxed a little bit, the calls go a lot better.

Beyond getting a few callbacks, we have call reluctance because we don't feel like we have a reason to call. A creative drop solves that problem. If I sent you a hooded sweatshirt or a Yeti cup, the reason for my call very simply is just to make sure you got it. While I've got you on the phone, I will also tell you why I sent it. That's really the reason for the call to see if you received it.

In the following chapter, we're going to talk about what we say when you get somebody on the phone which we call the "Three Asks." It dovetails very nicely with the creative drop. I sent the hooded sweatshirt to the USC graduate and said to the CFO, "If you don't mind, call me back. I want to make sure you got the sweatshirt and make sure you know why I sent it."

When they call me back, I tell them, "I wanted to make sure you received it. I wanted to make sure you know why I sent it because I work with CFOs of nonprofits (or whatever niche they are in), and I know you are one." So, we send a creative drop because of "who" they are. This will make more sense when we get to the Three Asks in the next chapter. The first ask for a meeting will be because of who they are, not because of what we do.

The Three Asks will make you confident about what you're going to say when you get people on the phone, but the creative drop can help get a lot of attention out of the call when you reveal too early in the typical sales call that you're a salesperson.

Look, you don't have to spend $100 on a creative drop, like the CFO that had the $1.5 million book of business. Reciprocity really just begins with someone seeing that you've gone to some trouble, and again, I'm more apt to call you back if there's some reason I want to reciprocate. But curiosity is probably worth twice as much as reciprocity. You may see on Facebook that they like fly fishing. You may see that they've run a half marathon. You may see there's a charity they believe in. All of these things we can find on social media and make for great creative drops.

The reason we call this a creative drop, the more creative it is, the better. It's something they've probably never received from anyone, much less from a salesperson.

Another great case study in creative drops is about a broker we worked with that didn't like the idea of creative drops, but she was part of a larger sales team that was routinely in a competition to see who could create the most appointments and she was not getting very far on her own.

She thought the creative drops were gimmicky, and we understood that the problem was the people in her office that were using them were getting far more appointments than she was. So we asked her this question: "Is there a creative drop that, if you received it, you wouldn't think was gimmicky? That you wouldn't think was cheesy?"

And she realized if somebody sent her a bottle of wine, she would not think that way and would probably return their call because of the gift.

So she found a vineyard that would etch people's names into the wine bottle. This is not fine wine from Napa or France, but good wine produced regionally. We were all amazed to learn that for every two bottles of wine she sent out, she got one appointment; she sent out 80 bottles of wine and yielded roughly 40 new business appointments.

This was somebody that hated the idea until she found one that made sense to her. And once she did, she was able to use this strategy to significantly ramp up prospecting and her new business production.

We have creative drops that are as cheap as a dollar that can be put in the U.S. mail. We have other clients, sales managers, that tell producers, "Hey, I'm gonna give you $3,000 for creative jobs. And every time you write a new business account, we're going to take a tiny percentage of the new business to pay for them." We have people consistently writing $400,000 a year in revenue that historically is only $100,000 or $150,000 because they were very good at what they did, but they just couldn't get enough people engaged.

The creative drop helped them blow up some call reluctance because it gave them a reason to call. It helped relax the person on the other end of the phone line but most importantly, it literally changed their career because they didn't have to call 20 people to get one person on the phone.

Hopefully, by now, you're starting to understand that creative drops can solve a lot of problems around cold calling.

There are some rules to creative drops that I think you have to understand. When talking to the gatekeeper, reference the creative drop. If you asked for Mr. Big and the gatekeeper asked you what this was regarding, you reference the Patagonia sweatshirt and say, "She'll know."

We want to be able to say, "She'll know" or "He'll know."

People always ask us, should we put our agency logo on the creative drop? The answer's no. We're not trying to use traditional marketing with this method. We are just trying to get a lot more people to call us back. We're trying to get people to call you back at a rate much better than the 20-to-one rate. People call us back because they're curious. Why did someone send me this?

So this is our best cold calling methodology. It will literally change your life if you figure this out for yourself. It solves many problems we face as prospectors.

There is one more prospecting method we would like to share with you. Again, we need to write another book on prospecting, but that's not what this book is about. We wanted to give you two of our unique methods to create many more new business appointments that we find easier to execute and, frankly, are a little more fun.

The second prospecting method is what we call "Running the R.O.O.T.A.," an acronym for <u>R</u>eferral <u>O</u>ut <u>O</u>f <u>T</u>hin <u>A</u>ir.

We made a decision a long time ago. We're not going to prospect 30 hours a week. We don't have time. We want to grow, and we want to leverage our time. We will get a few clients, serve them differently than they had been served before, and then ask them to introduce us to people they knew. That's how we built our business, and it worked.

Somewhere along the way, we started teaching people to do the same thing. You get some clients, and you'll over-serve those clients. You build a robust service calendar, you are consistent, you are unique and different, Blue Ocean, and they'll introduce you to people.

One reason so many people are not getting introduced is they're just average, and they're just like everybody else. But somewhere along the way, we ran into a problem. Look, we have a lot of really amazing clients. They are very good at what they do. We would consider them *Blue Ocean Advisors*. And here's what we learned.

Many times some of our best clients were not asking for referrals. And, you know why? Because they felt like it was putting undue pressure on the person they were asking, and since it put pressure on their client, then it put pressure on them, and so they just didn't ask. That's problem number one.

Problem number two is when we look to ask people for introductions, there's a limited universe of people we know that can actually introduce us: People who understand what we do and have experienced what we do. They're fabulous for an introduction model, and the same goes for CPAs, bankers, or lawyers.

This universe can just be a little bit small.

So, our big question was how can we come up with a way to get 80% of the result of an introduction from our client without putting pressure on them? So again, maybe not quite as good as our client introducing us to a prospect, but what if it's only 80% as effective? And we can do it 100 more times?

That's what the R.O.O.T.A. is about. You don't have to ask anybody for anything. You don't have to ask for their permission. We believe if you want to learn how to run the R.O.O.T.A. most efficiently and effectively, then you'll want to use LinkedIn Sales Navigator to simplify the process.

There are many tutorials out there, but a salesperson not leveraging Sales Navigator to see how you're connected to ideal prospects would be like a carpenter not having a hammer. It allows you to build a list of second-degree connections and is even more powerful if that can be done within your vertical. In case you didn't know, a second-degree connection would just be someone connected to one of your first-degree connections (someone you're connected with) that you aren't connected with.

Let us give you the simplest example of how to run the R.O.O.T.A. and explain why it's so effective.

There are two parts to the R.O.O.T.A.: The front half is purely doing research. And there's the back half, where we call and try to execute the referral. Back during Covid, when all our neighbors happened to be out in their front yards at night with their favorite libation, everyone was out walking and doing things of that nature. I stopped at the curb and asked my neighbor across the street, "Hey, Jay, how are Ashley and the girls," he let me know they were doing fine.

The prospect that I want to get in front of is Michael Bosworth in Tyler, Texas. Jay also lives in Tyler. I simply asked Jay, "Do you know Michael Bosworth?"

He said, "Yeah, I do."

I then asked, "Jay, what do you think about him?" And that's it.

That simple, I now have laid the groundwork to execute my referral out of thin air by doing nothing more than asking my neighbor what he thinks about my target prospect, Michael Bosworth.

So now, I can go back home on a Friday night, call Michael, and leave him a voicemail.

"Hey, Michael, this is Ad Visor, I don't know if you know me, but I live across the street from Jay and Ashley Ferguson. Your name came up tonight in a brief conversation, and anyway, I wanted to share it with you. Give me a call back on my cell when you have a moment."

Running the R.O.O.T.A. could literally be that easy and commonly is. The front half is asking somebody about your target prospect, in this case, Jay, about Michael. Now, why did I do that? Because I needed to create a story so I could call Michael and tell him, "Hey, Michael, your name came up." Now, if I wanted to, I could make that research piece much more robust when I call Michael.

Back to the lawn conversation with Jay.

I could ask Jay if he knows anything about what I do for a living.

I work with insurance brokers.

I do a lot of research on the prospects before I ever call them.

I'm researching a prospect right now named Michael Bosworth. I like to get as many opinions on them as I can. I am very picky about who I work with, and I don't call on everyone.

Now, I'm doing that because Michael may end up asking Jay Ferguson, my neighbor. Hey, what did Jeff talk about? Or when I leave Michael a voicemail, he may call Jay.

And if you want to get more in-depth on this research piece, although I think you don't have to, think about what your prospect may ask this person and try to have a conversation.

What I want him to tell Michael is that he does a lot of research on prospects and he was checking you out.

Now, I actually like the easier version. In the first version, I just asked him if he knew Michael. I asked him his opinion, and he told me he was a good guy. And then I just called and left that on the voicemail.

When we ask people in our workshops how many would call someone back if they left that voicemail, everyone agrees it's much better than one out of 20, and most agree more than half at least.

Now, it's also fun if the gatekeeper answers and asks me what this call is regarding. I say I live across the street from Jay Ferguson, and Jay was telling me about Michael a couple of days ago, and I'm just following up on that conversation.

Creative drops and running the R.O.O.T.A. solve a huge problem with the gatekeeper.

Remember earlier we talked about whatever creative drop you send when the gatekeeper asks, you say, "Just reference the Yeti Cup with the University of Texas logo on it. He'll know"?

Well, with the R.O.O.T.A., we say, "I'm following up on a conversation I had with my next-door neighbor, Jay Ferguson, about Michael."

If they give me a hard time, I just hang up, call back after hours, and leave them a voicemail. This gets much, much better when you leave more specifics on your voicemail. We can build a much more robust voicemail for us to leave if we build a backstory. We can cite who we were speaking to, where we were, when we were there, and what the occasion was to make this voicemail much more familiar and authentic. So, now when we call Michael Bosworth, we can say, "Michael, I was at Jay Ferguson's lake house out on Lake Tyler a couple of weeks ago. We were celebrating his wife Susan's 40th birthday. At some point in the night, your name came up. If you don't mind, give me a call. I want to share the conversation with you briefly."

So, the more you will tell people where you were, what time it was, what day it was, and what the event was, the more real you are.

Let us give you one more example of someone running the R.O.O.T.A. on Jeff and being good at it.

He called Jeff the day after Thanksgiving several years ago and said, "Hey, Jeff, your name just keeps coming up," He named the three people Jeff's name had come up with and said they were kind of in the same industry.

He said, "Hey, if you're ever in Fort Worth, I'd love to buy you lunch at the Fort Worth Club."

Well, that was a great idea to say that because the Fort Worth Club is a cool place, it's where the Davey O'Brien Award is given out. As a matter of fact, the day I met this young man for lunch, I heard Vern Lundquist, the famous announcer, in the background. It was the day Baker Mayfield was getting that award for the nation's best quarterback in February several years ago.

There's something important we want you to understand. Never in a million years would Jeff think to ask him who brought his name up. This person could have asked three people about Jeff, so he could call and say, "Jeff, your name just keeps coming up."

Why wouldn't we ever ask him who brought our name up?

It's because you're so flattered. In a million years, it would never occur to you that this person may have brought your name up to three people so that they could call you and say your name just keeps coming up.

Now, if somebody were to ask us if we did that, and someone were to ask us who brought their name up, we would tell them we did, but it just never comes up. It's an easy pivot.

Running the R.O.O.T.A. solves a couple of other problems worth mentioning before we close out the chapter.

Asking somebody to introduce you to someone else creates pressure. You don't need a CPA or a client to run the R.O.O.T.A. because we're just trying to get a callback. You can run the R.O.O.T.A. with anybody.

We could ask somebody that trims our yard, that babysits our kids, whose kids play ball with our kids, or anyone if they know our target prospect. It's about getting a callback.

All we have to do is bring their name up in a conversation so that we can call the prospect and let them know their name came up.

I can't tell you how many appointments we've had booked over the years between our clients and us, but it is staggering. It's honestly not a fair fight.

A record for appointments generated in one week from running the R.O.O.T.A. came from someone in our 2021 prospecting Ph.D. class who booked 17 appointments in one week because he got excited and learned how to execute the R.O.O.T.A. He ran the R.O.O.T.A. with three COIs, and it worked beautifully.

Another benefit of running the R.O.O.T.A. is that you get to control the timeframe. Someone may tell you they're going to make an introduction for you, but they never get around to it. But with this, you don't have to wait.

Once you ask Jay Ferguson about his neighbor Michael Bosworth, and he tells his opinion, it's "go time." You can call Michael at any point after that.

The final advantage of the R.O.O.T.A. is that you get to control what the buyer hears about you. We will not lead with what we do (broker), which is the ultimate non-starter. He may introduce us in a number of ways that we don't want to be introduced. The R.O.O.T.A. puts that power back in your hands.

And so we would encourage you to take us up on this and learn how to run the R.O.O.T.A. Whether it's creative drops or making cold calls that are running the R.O.O.T.A., this is the fastest way we know at Blueprint to get more opportunities into your pipeline.

Now, in the next chapter, we're going to talk about what you're going to say if somebody actually picks up the phone. Think about the compound effect of running the R.O.O.T.A. once a day, once a week, or once a month for the rest of your career. If you can do this 20 times, you may have as many as 15 people calling you back.

One of the reasons senior producers don't make cold calls is they don't have enough time to make 20 calls for one person to call them back. The R.O.O.T.A. will dramatically increase that, making these calls a lot warmer. You're borrowing the credibility; you're the person you're doing the research. And these calls just go much, much easier from the job.

One of our favorite things also about the R.O.O.T.A. is it's very social in nature. It should feel like a business play.

If you're in sales, you're probably fairly gracious socially. People who are good socially are good at running the R.O.O.T.A. If they're going out to a party, they want to make sure they meet a lot of people. Maybe they go on to LinkedIn and get connected with the people they met at the party and then see who those people know.

We can navigate our social lives, our kids' functions, really everywhere we live and work. You could be at little four-year-old Timmy's birthday party, and somebody's "name comes up." As you can see, it's not a fair fight.

When it comes to using your cadence to fill your pipeline, we would ask you to do this twice a week, once on Tuesday morning at nine and once on Thursday morning at nine. If you really want to step it up, invest one hour a week in running the R.O.O.T.A. and watch how your book of business blows up.

CHAPTER NINE

Pattern Interrupt & The Three Asks

What if every prospect you ended up on a call with asks you what you do? In this chapter, that's where we're headed.

The purpose of this chapter is to discuss how we can have an effective and meaningful first call with the prospect. It is our number one coaching request, as you might imagine, and hopefully, we proved in the last chapter that it might not actually be the most important coaching request we get, but it is definitely the most frequent.

That question is, *What can you give me to say to a prospect that will improve my chances of getting an appointment off of that conversation?*

We definitely believe there are things we can say and do that will produce a much better result. As we stated in Chapter 7, the typical conversion rate from conversation to appointment is five conversations will generate one appointment. Our goal with The Three Asks is to improve that metric.

We want you to have a lot of confidence when you start prospecting. We want you to be armed with a very effective conversation and for you to believe it is your best shot at getting an appointment. This particular skillset will help you be much more confident and reduce call reluctance.

One of our least favorite things about prospecting, especially the colder prospecting that we might be doing, is that moment when a prospect picks up the phone, we just let freedom ring. It makes us just like other salespeople, not just in the insurance world but any salesperson of any type. They wait for the prospect to pick up the phone and then get as much out as possible, hoping that something will stick out to the prospect and the prospect will want to know more.

Sadly, what really happens is that it triggers a response in the prospect that does not help us, and even worse is when we can sense that the prospect is irritated or at least disappointed that they got stuck on the phone with the salesperson. We can and will be able to eliminate that issue by simply using a pattern interrupt and The Three Asks.

Let us begin with talking about the pattern interrupt. The pattern interrupt is simply a tool that we can use so that we are not perceived as a typical salesperson in the opening moments of a sales call. If we use it correctly, we will be able to keep a prospect off balance and also keep them on the phone longer as they're trying to figure out who we are.

In Chapter 8, we discussed how we could approach prospects differently. This part of the prospecting process also needs to be different, and that's where the pattern interrupt comes into play. There are different types of pattern interrupts that we could use, and fortunately, when we're cold calling using a creative drop or running the R.O.O.T.A., the pattern interrupt is built in.

A simple pattern interrupt could be something like, "Hello, my name is Tom Johnson with ABC company. Does my company name ring a bell?"

That simple one is designed for us to avoid just talking fast to get out a lot of information quickly, hoping that something will stick. Another thing about that particular pattern interrupt is that they might not know if you are a client, so they have to stick with you a little bit longer. Every second a prospect stays on the phone helps us. We want to try and avoid their reflexive attempts to get us off the phone, especially in the early seconds of the call. Again, this is a simple pattern interrupt that we can use.

Another type of pattern interrupt that requires a little more skill and confidence (but is highly effective) is to, when the prospect picks up, say something like, "Oh, hi Bob, I wasn't expecting you to pick up the phone. I know you are super busy, and I did not intend to interrupt your day. Would you like me to call you back and leave you a voicemail?"

This seems counterintuitive, but if our goal is not to be perceived as a salesperson at all costs, and in some ways, it is, this is a very effective method to keep your prospect off balance. If they are really busy, we get to leave them a voicemail that can trigger a callback, and it actually helped us that we didn't try to force ourselves on them when they picked up the phone. We have used that particular pattern interrupt many times, and it has worked as well as any. Remember, we're trying to differentiate, and being non-pushy can differentiate you from other people.

An even more aggressive pattern interrupt that we have used many times is when your prospect picks up the phone and says something really bold like, "Hi Bob, my name is Tom, and this is a sales call. Do you want to hang up on me now?" (with a little chuckle)

I know that last one might not be comfortable for most of you, but we have used it many times over the years, and 99% of the time, the response is, "You know, actually, I do want to hang up, but since you were honest, go ahead."

An effective pattern interrupt allows us to slow everything else down on the call as we work through The Three Asks.

Let's talk about a pattern interrupt when we are using a creative drop. When we're using a creative drop, our pattern interrupt is about the actual creative drop itself. We would send Yeti mugs to people years ago and would commonly say as a joke, "I heard you could keep a beer cold for nine hours in that thing, but I haven't been able to make it to nine minutes." Then we could ask them if they had ever heard of a Yeti—if they had one or if they'd ever used one. The point is we would stay on the thing that we dropped on them as long as possible so this would not feel like a normal sales call and would set up the first ask nicely.

When we are doing a pattern interrupt while we are running the R.O.O.T.A., it is around the person that we have in common with the prospect that we're talking to. The more you know about the person you have in common, the longer you can talk about that person and build rapport and trust during that process. No matter what, it won't feel like a traditional salesperson calling someone they don't know.

Once you get really comfortable with a couple of different pattern interrupts you can use and be prepared with, it becomes easy to transition into The Three Asks.

The Three Asks is designed to slow everything down. We ask one question, and we wait for a response. We ask another question, wait for a response, and do that a third time before making a last-ditch effort. The Three Asks is methodical, and we are standing on solid ground the entire time.

As we get ready with the first of the three asks and as you begin to better understand the difference between a transactional Red Ocean Broker that looks like and talks like everyone else compared to a *Blue Ocean Advisor* who swims alone and is seen as different and valuable in a unique way, you will understand their focus.

A Red Ocean Broker focuses on themselves and their tools and products and pushes them out toward potential buyers hoping they will buy them. The core of their thinking is their "stuff."

A *Blue Ocean Advisor* focuses on the relationship with their ideal clients and prospects. Eventually, that may lead to tools and products but only after a thorough understanding of their situation. The core of their thinking is a relationship first; it is always about their client, not themselves.

Because we believe that is true, our first ask will be based on WHO we work with, not WHAT we do. As an example of what I mean, if someone were to ask a *Blue Ocean Advisor* what they do, their response would be, "I work with CFOs." That may seem odd to you at this point, but we're going to start with who we work with and work our way out to what we do for them.

The First Ask

Let's pick up this conversation on the first ask after we have done a creative drop; we have gotten a return call and discussed the creative drop as a pattern interrupt.

"Bob, let me explain why I sent that Yeti cup to you specifically. I work with CFOs, and I know you're the CFO of XYZ company. My goal is to set up a 20-minute meeting over the next couple of weeks to share with you some of the work my team and I are doing with the CFOs we work with."

Remember that a major reason that we're using the three asks is to slow this down and hopefully get them to ask us what we do. In this scenario, they might even think we forgot to tell them what we did. It's ok because, as we have found repeatedly, they will likely ask us, "What is it that you do for CFOs?" Which clearly is going to lead us to our second ask.

There are several reasons we want to lead with who we work with as the first ask. One is we want them to know they are the person we need to speak with. If you say to a prospect, we work with "business owners," at some point in the conversation, they might want to kick you down to someone else that really doesn't make the decision but possibly is an information gatherer that could keep you from getting back up the food chain later. We want to keep that from happening as much as possible, and this is one mechanism to help with that. We will be standing on solid ground when they try to kick us down, and we can tell them that what we created, we created for the business owner (or the CEO, CFO, or whomever), not HR or someone else lower on the decision tree.

We really want to make sure that everyone understands how critical this part of the process is. Nothing is worse than getting kicked down to someone who cannot tell you yes but can only tell you no. As a salesperson, you did everything right, except you had the wrong people in the room. Our goal is to make sure you get them in the room to begin with, and it will transform your closing ratios. Closing ratios have more to do with who you deal with than anything else. If we miss that piece, it doesn't matter how great the rest of your process is; you will lose too many deals.

The second ask has more to do with what you do. It's the reason they should meet with you. In the second ask, we want to make sure we push forward an outcome instead of a thing. We still want them to be curious enough to want to know more, so the goal is to lay out your value proposition in a way that they see it as something valuable but might not be sure what is behind it, and to find that out, they will need to meet.

We can talk through the second ask with or without revealing we are a broker too early. Let's try it first without leading with the fact that we are brokers.

The Second Ask

Remember the first ask was asking them to meet with you to walk you through what you do for CFOs. And they respond with something like, "Well, what do you do for CFOs?"

A response that doesn't lead with you calling yourself a broker could be, "I consult with CFOs to help them identify financial levers on their healthcare spend that brokers aren't talking about. Are you open to 20 minutes sometime over the next couple of weeks?"

I purposely try to keep them from blocking me with, "They are happy with their current broker." Even if they try, I'm prepared for it. "I want to discuss financial levers brokers aren't bringing to you."

Ask Two could be one of these:

"I consult with business owners to lower their total cost of risk and insurance premiums with unique loss modeling tools we have developed."

"I consult with business owners by benchmarking their insurance premiums against the highest-performing companies in their zip code."

"I consult with CFOs to help them trim the fat out of their healthcare plan, usually to the tune of 15-30%."

There are endless reasons for us to meet, and you need to come up with your favorite until it fits just right. A good way to know if you are on the right track is if they ask you to explain what you are talking about in more detail.

"What do you mean by financial levers?"

The Third Ask

This leads us to ask number three: We believe in using case stories, and we say stories instead of studies because they should be quick and meaningful. Every producer should have three in their pocket to use when they need them.

The response could be: "Let me give you an example of what I mean by a financial lever. I don't know if this is a financial lever that we will help you pull, but recently we took someone out of their fully insured Blue Cross plan, moved them to a reference-based pricing model, and saved them $600,000. Again, I don't know if that's a lever that we would help you pull, and we can't guess, but our process is designed to help us find the ones that will be the biggest opportunity for you. There are over 40 that we could pull from. Would you be open to meeting for 20 minutes over the next couple of weeks?"

P&C Response: "Well, I'm not sure if this is a financial lever, we will help you pull, and we can't guess what it will be, but recently we took a potential client through our process, and we were able to eliminate 40% of their workers' comp claims using a tool called nurse triage, one of the tools in our post-loss mitigation toolbox. Most people don't even know it exists because brokers aren't talking about it. Again, this is one out of roughly 40 different possible financial levers that you could pull. Would you be open to 20 minutes over the next couple of weeks to see what opportunities are available for you?"

If you're uncomfortable not leading with you are a broker in the second ask, then you can add that by simply saying, "I am a broker, but I am not calling to quote your insurance. I am sure you have a broker you are happy with. Is that correct?" They will likely answer yes to that or something similar to that.

Then we go right into the value proposition: "I thought so; most people are happy, but I am reaching out to discuss financial levers brokers aren't speaking about mainly because they don't understand it. It is the impact of data analytics on your

insurance cost and how to drastically lower premiums using predictive analytics. Has anyone spoken to you about this seismic shift in how insurance is underwritten? Would you be open to 20 minutes to see what opportunities are out there for you by leveraging a modern set of tools like this?"

Whether you lead with "I'm a broker" or wait on that part, it doesn't make a huge difference. It just depends on how "blue ocean" you want to go.

We have a huge database of these types of value propositions and case stories inside our program, and we would recommend that you build a database of these as well. It makes training new people much easier, and everyone in the organization will feel like they're on solid ground when they're out there talking to people about what makes you different.

Let's do a recap of Pattern Interrupt and The Three Asks.

The Pattern Interrupt is designed for you to be perceived as anything but a salesperson very early in the conversation so that you can build rapport and keep the prospect off-balance until your first ask.

Your **First Ask** is about who you work with—CFOs of Senior Living Facilities, Owners of Construction Companies, etc. The more industry-focused you can be, the better off you are.

Your **Second Ask** is about differentiating you from the typical broker by talking about things brokers aren't. The more your value is tied to benchmarking, unique financial levers, one-of-a-kind toolbox, etc., the more effective it will be for them to want more.

Your **Third Ask** is about using case stories to substantiate your claims of better outcomes. Each one creates an opportunity to ask for a twenty-minute meeting to see what opportunities exist for them. The simpler the premise, the more effective it will be. You don't want them to have too much to think about. We want them to ask themselves, *Do I want to know about unique financial levers that brokers aren't bringing me to lower my costs?*

As a last-ditch effort, we can ask them if they ever have someone take a look at their program, and if so, when would that be, and what can we do to be put on the list of people to help them evaluate it? I also like to tell them we typically start 90 days before anyone else does because some of the most effective financial levers can't be pulled if we wait too long.

Lastly, sometimes we just have to hang in there a little bit longer. That is where the mindset of being an effective prospector really comes into play.

We know we have presented a lot of information in this book with ideas that range from how to open a conversation, differentiating on a first appointment, getting them into a discovery meeting, and how to create value in your proposal in a unique way. We hope you have found the principles in this book meaningful and easy to follow, but more than that, we hope you join others on this journey of building a massive book of business by becoming a *Blue Ocean Advisor.*

THANK YOU FOR READING OUR BOOK!

DOWNLOAD YOUR FREE GIFTS

Just to say thanks for buying and reading our book. We would like to give you a few free bonus gifts, no strings attached!

To Download Now, Visit:
www.BlueOceanAdvisorBook.com/Blueprintgifts

We appreciate your interest in our book, and value your feedback as it helps us improve future versions. We would appreciate it if you could leave your invaluable review on Amazon.com with your feedback. Thank you!

Made in the USA
Columbia, SC
27 October 2024

7e14241a-dde3-4f10-afc8-34c691ea8f97R01